Top of the Order

Top *of the* Order

25 Writers Pick Their Favorite
Baseball Player of All Time

Sean Manning

EDITOR

DA CAPO PRESS
A Member of the Perseus Books Group

Set in 11 point Arno Pro by the Perseus Books Group

Library of Congress Cataloging-in-Publication Data

Top of the order : 25 writers on their all-time favorite baseball player / Sean Manning, editor. — 1st Da Capo Press ed.
   p. cm.
   Includes bibliographical references.
   ISBN 978-0-306-81855-4 (alk. paper)
   1. Baseball players—United States. 2. Baseball—United States—History. I. Manning, Sean.
   GV865.A1T65 2010
   796.357092'2—dc22

                          2009053844

Published by Da Capo Press
A Member of the Perseus Books Group
www.dacapopress.com

Da Capo Press books are available at special discounts for bulk purchases in the U.S. by corporations, institutions, and other organizations. For more information, please contact the Special Markets Department at the Perseus Books Group, 2300 Chestnut Street, Suite 200, Philadelphia, PA 19103, or call (800) 810-4145, ext. 5000, or e-mail special.markets@perseusbooks.com.

10 9 8 7 6 5 4 3 2 1

CONTENTS

Jim Rice

Mariano Rivera

FOREWORD

W. P. Kinsella

I've seen many baseball superstars in whom I have no interest at all; I don't get excited about their performance, no matter how spectacular. Some I'm simply indifferent to; some I actively dislike. But why? There have been marginal players I've admired, journeymen I looked forward to seeing, sometimes driving a few hundred miles out of my way to attend a game of theirs. But why?

I can't imagine being able to expound on one player's merits for a whole essay. If I did, that player would be Curt Flood. He had to be one of the bravest men who ever lived. At the end of a marvelous career, the three-time All-Star took on the stodgy and often mean-spirited baseball establishment, challenging the reserve clause that tied a player to one team for life. In a most iffy decision the Supreme Court found in favor of Major League Baseball, but Flood had put the wheels of change in motion, and the clause was struck down in 1975, opening the doors of free agency and allowing baseball players to earn whatever the market would bear.

It seems that being a fan or nonfan of a player is completely subjective. For instance, I've always considered that Willie McGee and Mickey Rivers were two sides of the same coin. Both were All-Star players, both had a shambling gait that could be elevated to blinding speed. Rivers spoke in malapropisms, some of them intentional; McGee was more articulate and probably the better of the two players. However, while I loved McGee, I never cared for Rivers. It probably had to do with McGee playing for my National League favorites, the Cardinals, while Rivers spent time with the hated Yankees and the uninteresting Texas Rangers.

My introduction to baseball was odd to say the least. My dad had played some minor-league baseball in Florida and California, probably only in commercial leagues in the 1920s. He was never terribly forthcoming about where he actually played, though his friends confirmed that he was a very good third baseman and a strong left-handed hitter. My dad was near forty when I was born, and I never saw him play ball. Through a series of somewhat strange events, too complicated to get into, he had ended up in Alberta, Canada, where I was born, settled on a stony and worthless quarter-section of farmland to wait out the Great Depression. On the rare occasions when he got to the nearest city, Edmonton, he would return with a copy of the St. Louis *Sporting News,* which I believe cost 5¢, and I remember him reading me articles about big-league ballplayers and explaining box scores to me, long before I started school.

The first players who interested me came from the black-and-white pages of the *Sporting News.* I had to provide my own color. And I did, for I became a fan of two colorful teams: the Cincinnati Reds and the St. Louis Cardinals. I have always loved bright colors; in fact, I'm wearing a cardinal-red corduroy shirt as I sit typing this essay. I imagined the Cincinnati players in red socks, red caps, and with red lettering on their shirts. I loved the perky cardinal perched on a bat on the St. Louis uniforms.

It was names that captured my imagination: the exotic and mysterious Cincinnati, their pitchers Bucky Walters and Johnny Vander

Meer. I had only the vaguest idea of what a no-hit game was, but my
father assured me that Vander Meer's back-to-back no-hitters was a
record that would never be equaled or surpassed. Then there was Ewell
"The Whip" Blackwell, what an awe-inspiring name, and a story about
him was accompanied in the *Sporting News* by a very bad black-and-
white photo, showing his unique sidearm delivery. The first position
player I admired was Grady Hatton, an average third baseman with a
.254 lifetime average over a twelve-year major-league career. I became
a fan because I loved his name, which my dad assured me made him
as Irish as we were.

By the time I was ten we had moved to Edmonton, and I rushed to
the box scores every day in the *Edmonton Journal* to see how my pitching and hitting heroes had fared. The first World Series I remember
clearly was 1946. Here were the Red Birds against the Red Sox; I chose
the Cardinals. There was no TV, and the World Series games were the
only baseball broadcasts we received on our battery radio in back-
country Alberta. I chose pitcher Harry "The Cat" Brecheen as my favorite, mainly because of his name and my fondness for cats. I also
loved the unusualness of the name Enos "Country" Slaughter, especially after he scored from first base on a single with the winning run
in Game Seven. I was never a fan of Ted Williams, though he was a
great player.

In 1948 I became an instant fan of Lou Boudreau the day he got
four hits, including two home runs, as Cleveland beat Williams and
the Red Sox 8–3 in a one-game playoff for the American League pennant. We didn't get a radio broadcast, but got a radio summary at the
end of each inning as the information came in over the wires.

It would be twenty years before I saw a major-league game in person,
so to that point all my favorites were chosen from newspapers, magazines, World Series radio broadcasts, and, after the mid-'50s, World Series TV (though until the mid-'60s TV quality was quite inferior).

I remember Don Larsen's no-hitter in 1956. We didn't yet have a TV, so I rode a streetcar far across the city to the University of Alberta student union, where there was a grainy black-and-white TV that reran the game late in the evening. The reception was so bad that the radio broadcast I'd listened to earlier in the day was superior, except for the jubilation of the players after the no-hitter was accomplished.

Except for that brief moment, I was never a Yankees fan. Their uniforms weren't colorful; they bought their pennants. One of the hardest adjustments I had to make was when Charlie Finley dismantled the Oakland A's: Ungrateful fans had failed to fill the stadium after Finley brought them world championships, and he shipped my favorite Reggie Jackson off to the Yankees, where I could never cheer for him again.

A player can go from hero to pariah in an instant. I remember writing of Robbie Alomar that he "floated like an angel above second base" while making an astonishing catch in the World Series against Philadelphia. I lost complete respect for Alomar the day he spit in the face of the fine umpire John Hirschbeck. That one action cost Alomar thousands of fans and killed any chance he ever had of being a Hall of Famer.

Gene Tenace was another favorite of mine because he was a clutch hitter and an intelligent and gritty catcher, even though he had only a .241 lifetime average. I was thrilled in 2008 to see Cito Gaston (one of my favorite managers, along with Dick Williams) bring Tenace in as hitting coach with Toronto, where I'm sure he doesn't put up with many .241 hitters.

I admired Finley's willingness to take chances; he brought a rather stodgy game kicking and screaming into modern times. He is responsible for the designated-hitter rule, which I think is the best thing ever and should be adopted by the National League. He dressed his players in glorious color, which had been so lacking in baseball and which has since been adopted by many teams in both leagues. Even though he was known as "Cheap Charlie" and many of his innovations failed, he paid his players to grow mustaches. (Remember Rollie Fingers? I think that mustache made his career.) As an owner Finley left a lasting legacy and someday that legacy will be recognized and he'll be in the Hall of Fame.

I saw my first live major-league game in San Francisco in 1966, an early-season game at a bitterly cold Candlestick Park, where two of the greatest pitchers of the era, Don Drysdale and Juan Marichal, faced off. Drysdale won.

I liked the Dodgers, but I was a careerlong fan of right fielder Ron Fairly, the reason being one of proximity. During college hiatus Ron spent a summer playing minor-league baseball for the Edmonton Eskimos in my hometown. I watched him play many times in tiny Renfrew Park, where the players were close enough for the fans to touch and talk to and get autographs. I followed his career with the Dodgers with interest, and to a lesser extent when he was with Montreal, one of my least favorite teams.

I saw my first live no-hitter in 1955. A pitcher named Kirby Pain pitched it for the Eskimos in what would probably be a Class C league, though I believe it was unaffiliated. He made me a fan for life, and I'm sad to report that he didn't go on to a major-league career, but fifty-five years later I still recall the thrill of that first no-hitter. I saw Bob Forsch pitch one in St. Louis many years later, missing a perfect game against Montreal when he intentionally plunked Gary Carter in his first at bat for some offense Carter had allegedly committed in a previous game.

Speaking of Montreal, I had never been a fan of Pete Rose; always considered him too brash and competitive to a fault. I will never forget how he ruined Ray Fosse's career by crashing into him, not in any crucial situation but in a meaningless All-Star Game. Then, I believe in the same series as Forsch's no-hitter, I watched as Rose laid down the perfect bunt, about twenty-five feet down the third-base line, landing soft and dying as if the ball was made of sponge cake. Rose was across first base without a throw, and my appreciation of him was elevated 1,000 percent, and because of that one play I was a fan the rest of his career. I was sorry to see the trouble that followed him, and I think he should be forgiven and allowed into the Hall of Fame.

When times are tough, one takes a hero anywhere one can find one. And Bombo Rivera was an unlikely hero. He was a platoon outfielder with Minnesota in the late '70s, an all-round average player except for his name. Minnesota had a pitiful team in those years, and I lived in Iowa and traveled frequently to Minnesota for whole home stands. The fans loved Bombo (a great trivia question would be: What was Bombo Rivera's given name? A: Jesus) and chanted his name every time he came to bat or made a play in the outfield. Chanting "Bombo! Bombo! Bombo!" (which, incidentally, means "fly ball") was a wonderful distraction from watching Minnesota lose game after game, and earned Bombo the respect and admiration of many fans. His major-league career was short, a brief stint with Kansas City after Minnesota, then he returned to Puerto Rico and later became a star in Japan for a couple of years. I mentioned Bombo in my novel *Shoeless Joe,* and Garrison Keillor wrote a song called "The Ballad of Bombo Rivera."

What to do when you are a fan of a particularly wretched team? In the '80s I lived in proximity to Seattle and for a couple of seasons attended almost all home games. I likened being a Seattle fan to loving a sick pet. You don't kick your cat because it hurls hairballs onto your favorite rug. I often attended mainly to see the opposition and to hope for an occasional miracle, like the night when, with the Mariners down two runs in the last of the ninth, Phil Bradley hit a three-run homer for the win. In those years you could count the miracles on the thumbs of both hands. However, if you watch a team long enough you develop favorites, no matter how inept the team as a whole may be.

My favorite Mariner, probably of all time, was second baseman Jack Perconte; he was a gritty little left-handed hitter, and a fair fielder who always made that extra effort, even if it ended in failure. I was almost attacked once when I suggested that Perconte was a better second baseman than his eventual successor Harold Reynolds. I admit in my heart that my attacker was probably right, but I'll stick with Perconte; that's what having a favorite player is all about. I never jumped on the Ken Griffey Jr. bandwagon. Certainly he was a great player, but my feeling has always been, right or wrong, that he too often failed to produce in the clutch, sometimes looking to me as if he wasn't trying very hard.

On that pitiful Seattle squad I also liked shortstop Spike Owen, but for an entirely different reason. Owen was an average player in all respects, but almost every game, sometimes several times a game, he fouled pitches straight back into the third deck behind home plate, where I sat. Crowds were sparse, and I soon collected more baseballs than I knew what to do with. It got so at the beginning of each game I picked a child nearby and would give him or her the ball if I collected one.

Who have I missed? I loved Bob Gibson, the growly superstar pitcher of the Cardinals. (An even better trivia question would be: What was Bob Gibson's given name? A: Pack.) He didn't care who was at bat; as far as he was concerned he owned the plate and brushed back everyone without discrimination. It is said that once when All-Star catcher Tim McCarver went to the mound, Gibson told him to get back behind the plate. "The only thing you know about pitching," he said, "is that you can't hit it." I'm afraid that at that point I would have pulled a Crash Davis (the veteran catcher from *Bull Durham*) and informed the next few hitters of exactly what pitch was coming their way. However, the crotchety Gibson was the best Cardinal pitcher ever. He holds records in almost every field of pitching and was a shoo-in for the Hall of Fame.

Of active players, Cy Young Award winner Roy Halladay is my favorite. He is tough and works quickly, and, while in Toronto, he managed to win despite the team's generally lackadaisical hitting.

What if I could meet one of my favorite players, just to say thank you for giving me many hours of pleasure at the ballpark? I've met a few in my day, but the talent of baseball players lies in their on-field exploits, just as mine consists of what I type onto manuscript pages. My life is not interesting; most ballplayers, when off the field, are not very colorful. I like the ones who were colorful both on and off the field.

I was once invited by a sports magazine to travel for a week with the Montreal Expos and write a profile of the team. I knew there were writers who would kill for such an opportunity, but I declined. What in the world would I have said to them? Most of them would have had no idea who I was: Baseball players are not the great readers of America. Another time I was asked by a Japanese magazine to interview Hideo Nomo, the herky-jerky Japanese star pitcher. They flew me to Los Angeles, where I was to catch up with him. I tried frantically to think of questions I could ask him. The only ones I could come up with were about sumo (I am a knowledgeable fan). If he wasn't a sumo fan, there would be a terribly long pause in the interview. Happily, while I was in the air, Nomo changed agents and all interviews were canceled. I have seldom felt such relief.

I'm fond of nonconformists, have always considered myself one, but in baseball, still a bastion of conservative thought, nonconformists are rare. My wife is not a baseball fan at all, but she remembers Luis Tiant because of his peculiar pitching motion, and so do I. He spent as much time looking at second base as he did his catcher.

The old-time players from my era—I'm talking 1940s to the '60s— were always tough and often mean. We'd have nothing to say to each other. Today's players listen to ear-splitting music by many "artists" I think should be in jail. (I guess I'm showing my age.) We'd have nothing to say to each other.

I have often told audiences that stamina accounts for about 85 percent of writing success. Therefore, I've always admired "The Old Gringo" George Brunet, who had some thirty major- and minor-league connections before he landed with the Angels for a few years. Hitters always seemed to forget they had bats when Brunet pitched. He twice led the American League in losses, despite a very respectable ERA each year. After the majors, Brunet pitched for years, well into his fifties in the Mexican leagues, and holds the minor-league strikeout record with 3,175 Ks. Now *that's* stamina.

I guess the person I'd like to spend a few hours with is the ever entertaining, completely unpredictable Bill "Spaceman" Lee. He was a great player who did things in his unconventional way. He threw the occasional eephus ball (probably learned from Tiant), a high-arching softball-like pitch that paralyzed many a hitter, but not Tony Perez, who hammered one out of the park in the 1975 World Series. I've heard Lee speak; he is articulate, literate, and side-splittingly funny, as talented as any stand-up comedian alive.

Favorites, it seems, come in all shapes, sizes, and degrees of talent. Years ago, when my twenty-something daughter traveled with me to a lot of games, she chose her favorite by how well his buns filled out his uniform pants. A totally acceptable way of choosing a favorite player, and I don't doubt that there are many fans of both sexes who still do the same.

Incidentally, her favorite was Kansas City catcher Jamie Quirk.

INTRODUCTION

Sean Manning

The congressional hearings. The Mitchell Report. Roger Clemens and Brian McNamee on Capitol Hill. A-Rod's contract negotiations. A-Rod's steroid revelations. Manny's contract negotiations. Manny's steroid revelations. The steady decline in African American players. (In 2008, barely a tenth of Major League Baseball was black—and that was the highest percentage since 1995.) Add to that the fact that even amid the worst economic downturn this country has experienced since the Great Depression, nearly half the league's teams opted to increase ticket prices for 2009—most egregiously the Yankees, who despite being baseball's richest club in 2008 by a mile (*Forbes* valued the team at $1.5 billion, making it the only organization to crack ten figures) and receiving in excess of a billion dollars in public financing for the construction of a new stadium, had the stones to jack up the cost of "nonpremium" seats a collective 76 percent over 2008 rates and initially charge as much as $2,650 for "premium" ones. (After a month of scarce turnout and vilification by local media and politicians, Yankee ownership came down on the latter price tag: As of this writing, sitting behind home plate now only runs you a measly $1,250.)

No, it hasn't been easy being a baseball fan these last few years—not even for those, as Christopher Sorrentino describes himself in his essay on Dave Kingman, "patently uninterested in journalists' concepts of the moral schema of the game as transgressed against by players." And yet the sport's popularity has hardly waned. In March 2008, the all-time record for single-game attendance was shattered when nearly 116,000 fans turned out to the Los Angeles Coliseum for an exhibition between the Dodgers and the Red Sox. In July of that year, the All-Star Game at the old Yankee Stadium scored the highest ratings ever for its Home Run Derby telecast—which, shown on ESPN, was also cable TV's highest-rated program for the entire year. The Midsummer Classic itself attracted more viewers than in the previous five years, earning it the top spot in that week's Nielsen ratings. And despite the recession, through the first month and a half of the 2009 season, attendance was down from 2008 by only about 5 percent overall, while ten of the thirty teams saw their gates rise.

I've heard it argued that the recession is, in fact, to be credited for this resiliency—that in tough, uncertain times such as these, people crave entertainment and diversion more than ever. But what's more responsible, I think, is the fans' relationship with the players. Counting spring training, the regular season, All-Star festivities, and the playoffs (should our team be fortunate enough), we spend nearly two hundred days out of the year with these guys. That's more time than a lot of us spend with our loved ones. And although Darin Strauss is doubtless right when he contends in his essay on Mariano Rivera that the bulk of today's players "would probably not like you if you [knew] them, and vice versa, because they're mostly egomaniacal multimillionaires who've had no education or socializing influence in their lives," that's precisely what they seem—friends, family even. In fact, I'd argue their astronomical salaries and exorbitant self-regard and boneheaded attempts to beat the system only heighten this impression. I mean, who doesn't have that one big-shot uncle or cousin who lords it over everyone that he drives a Benz and lives in a McMansion of the sort Whitney Pastorek depicts in her essay on Clemens, or that scamming hustler buddy from childhood who's always concocting one ultimately ill-fated scheme or another? Granted, it usually doesn't involve injecting themselves with a women's fertility drug or committing perjury before a federal grand jury, but you get the idea.

And of course, just as with loved ones, when it comes to ballplayers, we may hold many of them dear to our hearts but can't help having one favorite. For a few of the contributors, theirs really were or still are friends . . . friends and teammates and mentors. (And business partners, as in the case of Roger Kahn, whose account of Jackie Robinson's rarely acknowledged foray into magazine publishing is evidence of how Robinson even now remains grossly underappreciated.) For the rest, however—it's no coincidence that there are twenty-five in total, the same number of players as on an active roster, nor that Rickey Henderson leads things off and Rivera closes—the bases for their biases, like most lay fans', is by and large more complicated. For some, it centers on class; for others, race. For some, it has to do with being of a similar age and the accompanying, as Strauss puts it, "intimations of mortality"; for others, it lies in the definitions of rebellion and conformity and the prospect of the two ever coexisting. A few contributors picked players they despised at first only to develop an affinity for in time, and a couple chose those they revered initially yet have grown to loathe—or at least to wonder at the discrepancy between their on-field personas and off-field realities. And then there are those whose fondness springs in part from afro circumference, model citizenry, imagined vengeance exacted on prepubescent tormentors, and, yes, absolutely, facial hair. Whatever the reason, each contributor sheds a little light on what it means to be beset by this strange torment of ours, this bizarre compulsion, this incurable malady known as baseball fandom.

The next few years aren't bound to be any easier for those of us afflicted. As long as the economy stays in the toilet and owners remain avaricious—both a pretty safe bet for some time to come—ticket prices will only keep climbing. (The discount on Yankees premium seats was for the 2009 season alone, and by late April the team had already announced an additional 4 percent hike in 2010.) The current labor agreement expires after the 2011 season, and those negotiations are likely to be contentious, since they'll be the first run by Michael Weiner, the newly appointed successor to Donald Fehr as executive director of the Players Association. Human nature being what it is, it's hard to envision the owners not looking to take advantage of Weiner's inexperience, and likewise to imagine he won't be overeager to prove he can't be pushed around. Plus, after A-Rod and Manny, there are still 102 names on the list of players who failed the 2003 "confidential" drug testing—now in possession of federal investigators. Go ahead and make that 100 names, following leaks about Sammy Sosa and David Ortiz. Who knows who else will have been exposed by the time this book hits the shelves?

Which just makes essays such as these all the more necessary, meant as they are to restore some of the faith in and love for the game you may have lately lost, to serve as a reminder that there's a hell of a lot more about it to cherish than to deplore, and most of all to celebrate those players who won us over and made us fans in the first place. The ones in whom we maybe see a little of ourselves, or perhaps the selves we'd like to be. The ones we pull for despite the ups and downs, with whom we win and lose, who may not be the best but who are, as Craig Finn states in his essay on Kirby Puckett, our guys.

And anyway, if you really think about it, when has following baseball ever failed to grate the conscience? Not in those years immediately following the Black Sox scandal, I guarantee you. Nor for a while there after the Rose ban. Not during the five strike seasons or the three lock-outs. And *especially* not during all those years of segregation. I, for one, am glad being a fan isn't easy—after all, as those players included in the Mitchell Report and that '03 list would've done well to remember, nothing worthwhile ever is.

Rickey Henderson				
STEVE ALMOND	◇	◇	◇	

We have to begin with the batting stance, because the stance is the ballplayer's signature, and because there has never been, in the history of the game, a stance as strange and devastating as that assumed—no fewer than 13,346 times over twenty-five seasons—by Rickey Henley Henderson.

To the uninitiated it looked utterly implausible, because Rickey was not standing. He was reclining. Or, more precisely, he was leaning back, a bit rakishly, on what at first appeared to be a massive bar stool, which (upon further inspection) revealed itself as a human leg—to wit, Rickey's own right leg, canted sharply at the knee.

The overall effect was deeply disconcerting to opposing pitchers. Although Rickey was listed at five foot ten in the programs, he barely topped four feet at the plate. He compressed the y-axis of the traditional strike zone—measured from knees to chest—to approximately a thumb's length.*

---

* The scribe Jim Murray once joked that Rickey's strike zone was "smaller than Hitler's heart." With all due respect to Mr. Murray's enthusiasm, it would be difficult to conceive of a more offensive metaphor.

If this makes Rickey sound like a ludicrous figure, a Quasimodo in cleats, I have done him wrong. Even in his contorted state, Rickey managed to look intimidating. His arms and legs were massive and richly braided with muscle. His trunk appeared carved from pig iron. As he waited for a pitch, he often waved his bat over the plate like a child's wand. He was not crouched so much as coiled.

This became clear the moment he initiated his swing. That swing! What furious ballet! What elegant violence! Rickey rising up from his bar stool and rocking forward in a controlled lunge, the bat zinging like a whipcord, all that torque and sprung rhythm inflicted upon the ball by means of a delectable crack, a frozen rope over the left field wall, say, which meant Rickey had occasion to pause at the plate and admire his handiwork, to tap his chest with the heels of his palms and crow, "That's what Rickey just did," before trotting toward first, where, taking a wide leisurely turn, he would execute a dainty hop step, as if to engage the base in a sultry South American dance of love.

Or maybe the ball had a bit less pepper on it and went merely screaming into the gap, in which case Rickey would set off in genuine haste, the very serious business of acceleration being his desired specialty.

This, too, was something opposing players did not want to see, particularly if you had the poor fortune to be stationed at third base: Rickey's body—the body of an NFL running back—circling wide around second, happily neglecting the stop sign being frantically flashed by the coach in the box behind you and hurtling helmet-first toward your fragile ankles at the approximate speed of sound.

He was probably safe; you were not.

But this is making certain assumptions, chiefly that Rickey would decide to swing at all. Often, he simply waited for the pitcher to misplace his composure and issue the walk. At which point (as Rickey might put it) *Rickey showed what Rickey was truly about.*

And you can rest assured, gentle reader, that you will find no one within the pantheon of belles lettres or beyond more devoted to Rickey's larcenous activities than your humble correspondent. I was there, after all, from the very beginning, a scrawny Little League burnout living an hour south of the Oakland Coliseum, where the Athletics made camp.

This would have been the summer of 1979. The epic teams of the early decade, winners of three straight World Series, were ancient history. The current roster was on its way to another sort of epic season, one in which they would win precisely a third of their games. They had announced their futility with gusto by going 5–24 in the month of June.

But I was and am one of those fans for whom the miseries of loyalty are impossible to resist. No matter how low the A's sunk, I found reasons to root for them. And thus, by that strange karmic covenant to which all devout fans (in their misshapen hearts) subscribe, at the franchise's absolute nadir, fate delivered me Rickey.

He went two for four in his debut, with a stolen base. I listened to that game on my trusty Panasonic radio. I saw him for the first time a few days later, during one of Oakland's rare televised contests. I was instantly and violently transfixed. It wasn't just the crazy stance or the preening manner or the freakish marriage of bulk and speed, but the powerful sense that you *had* to watch Rickey, because if you didn't you were going to miss something unprecedented.

This is the first and final signifier of stardom: that your presence on the field suggests possibility. Because possibility—some new miracle carved from air, some abrupt confrontation between grace and peril— is the reason we watch sports. Michael Jordan had it. Wayne Gretzky.

Barry Sanders. The British footballer Paul Gascoigne. And Rickey—the stuff came off him like sparks.

It went without saying that he was going to get on base at least once every game, either via hit or walk, fielder's choice, hit by pitch—whatever it took. And once he had one base, hey, you might as well have handed him second, heavily braised in gall. That first half-season he amassed thirty-three thefts. The following year Billy Martin took over as manager, and Rickey qua Rickey was born.

Martin was a believer in the art of disruption, a hothead who functioned best amid improvised tumult. Rickey stole one hundred bases in 1980.

It was a satisfying ritual to witness. There was, to begin with, the Rickey Lead, never less than five generous paces. Most base stealers will lean or even hope to be swaying as they break toward second. Rickey remained motionless, locked in a predatory squat, his fingers twitching above the infield dirt, his gaze fixed on the pitcher's elbows.

He radiated not just menace, but immense patience. The pitcher might throw to first half a dozen times. On each occasion, Rickey would dive back and dust himself off, then take the exact same lead. Eventually, the pitcher would have to deliver the ball home—the game's progress required him to do so.

Rickey was generally three steps into his steal by the time this happened. He ran like a sprinter, low and wide, his thighs rippling beneath his trousers.* It took him less than three seconds to travel those seventy-

---

* No ballplayer ever wore his pants tighter than Rickey. I often wondered if, like a matador, he had to be lowered into them. And I also wondered if one of his many tics—the plucking of the fabric at the crease of his crotch—was a result of this snug fit. In the end, it struck me as more likely the result of a desire to call attention to his considerable genital bulge.

five feet, a smooth churning that culminated with the Rickey Crash Landing. The problem of deceleration was solved, rather ingeniously, by means of friction: his body sliding across the bag slowed him down; the toes of his cleats hooked on the front edge of the base kept him from proceeding into left field.

As a manager, Billy Martin was many things. Irascible. Drunken. Mercurial. But he was not stupid. His strategy with the A's was simple: Give Rickey the green light and let fly. The results bore him out. In two seasons, the A's vaulted from the cellar to the pennant. The following year, Rickey blew past every known record by stealing 130 bases. He had 84 by the All-Star break. (To put this in historical perspective—no player has stolen that many bases in an entire season since 1993, when Rickey tallied 93.)

He would go on to lead the league in steals for the next seven seasons, and eleven of the next twelve. In 1998, at the age of thirty-nine, he led the league a final time. Over the course of his career—which stretched into 2004—he was thrown out in less than one-fifth of his attempts.

It's impossible to convey how sick this figure is. After all, everyone in the stadium knew Rickey was going to steal. The pitchers and catchers and bemused shortstops were doing everything in their power to stop him. He wound up with 1,406 steals, shattering Lou Brock's mark of 938.*

Even more astonishing is the fact that 796 of the 2,190 walks Rickey collected in his career came when he was leading off an inning. You really need to think about what this means. Because if you were an

---

* He tied Brock's record on a Sunday in April 1991, and a few innings later, amid a growing din, he broke for second again. The umpire called him out. But I was at that game, high up on the first-base side, and I can tell you without fear of bias that our man was safe.

opposing pitcher facing Rickey Henderson, and he was the first man up in the inning, what's the one thing, above all else, you *would not* do? You wouldn't walk him. You wouldn't issue him a free pass to harass you, to humiliate your catcher, to tie your infield into knots.

Which just goes to show that among his more flagrant gifts was a preternatural sense of his own strike zone as interpreted by particular umpires, the capacity to stay his bat as a fastball strayed an inch or two outside, and to protect the plate. Rickey the Heathen was, in fact, religiously disciplined as a hitter.

I'm not a great believer in stat porn, and so you will excuse me if I skip the rest of the assorted Rickey Records. You can look those up. I'd prefer to speak briefly about his legacy and specifically the reputation he has acquired over the years as a figure of comic self-regard.

Cue the Rickey Lore . . .

- *Rickey falls asleep on an ice pack and gets frostbite.*
- *Rickey receives a $1 million bonus from the A's and hangs the check on his wall without depositing it.*
- *Rickey hits a dinger and slides into home.* *

There are dozens of such tales floating around, some of them actually true. They cast Rickey as a narcissistic nincompoop, a dumb jock, the ultimate hot dog. As such, they represent a deeply condescending and vaguely racist perspective that draws a thick line between physical prowess (i.e., "That boy sure can run!") and presumably genuine forms of intelligence.

---

* In his defense, this *was* the run that broke Ty Cobb's career record for runs scored.

I will tender no argument, however, in the matter of temperament. Rickey *was* a cocky bastard. He boasted incessantly and referred to himself in the third person, often while gazing at himself nude in the mirror. He flicked his mitt at fly balls. And so on.

But if we're going to record this, we should also acknowledge the curious truth that greatness requires a certain insolence. This has been true since the days of Achilles. The spoils of historical regard go to those willing to step out in front of the battle lines and challenge the gods directly.

That Rickey did so, and that he talked about his ability to do so, only makes him a more honest version of every other professional athlete on earth. They are all raging egomaniacs, regardless of whatever aw-shucks team-first nonsense they spew for the microphones. You don't get to The Show by hiding your light under a bushel.

But Rickey's persona has too often obscured the shocking and subtle acumen of his play. Baseball, after all, is a game of small efficiencies, and no one has ever exploited these as assiduously as Rickey. Long before chemically aided homers became the league's star attraction and sabermetrics its church doctrine, Rickey was converting 1–2 counts into walks, which became de facto doubles. He acted like a clown, but the joke was on you if you missed what was actually happening. He was paying closer attention to the game than anybody else.

Rickey also suffered, as most athletes do, by staying at the party too long. He became a figure of unintended pathos, grumbling for a contract at age forty-five, unwilling to wander quietly out to pasture. Even as he entered the Hall of Fame in the summer of 2009, he sounded itchy for a comeback. Well, why the hell not? I'd take an arthritic Rickey over half the palookas on the A's current roster.

But I am happiest to remember Rickey in those first few years with Oakland, before he began pinballing around the league as a hired gun, before he returned to an A's squad plumped on steroids, before his audacious feats came to feel routine.

Sometimes at night, when my wife and babies are sleeping and I'm lying in a dark house knotted up with the anxieties of domestication, I close my eyes and Rickey comes to me. He is absently patrolling left field with his gap-toothed grin. Or scrunched impossibly over home plate. But most of the time he is sliding himself into position off first base.

He sets his elbows atop those massive thighs; his gloved fingers twitch just above the red dirt. He stares hard at the pitcher, that poor sod, and I can feel it: the electrical impulse that joins all fans to their favorite players, that makes the chest buzz with the strange, resounding love we offer those who enact our bodily dreams. And all I can think is this: *Rickey's gonna go, Rickey's gonna go.* It's like a chant, soothing and childish, something that pleads to be uttered out loud.

But before that can happen, Rickey's gone.

Tom Seaver

PAT JORDAN

I called Tom recently to ask for a favor. We haven't spoken much in the past ten years. He's retired, living on his estate surrounded by his vineyard in Northern California. I'm still working, living in a little Key West cottage in Fort Lauderdale. Our ships don't pass much anymore, in the night or the day.

In our twenties, thirties, and forties, we used to talk a lot . . . oh, maybe not a lot, not *every* day, but often enough. We'd talk at his barnlike home in Greenwich, Connecticut, down the road from my home in Fairfield, when we were in our late twenties, early thirties. We sat outside on his porch on a sunny summer's day. Tom cooked us steaks on his barbeque grill, the big tenderloin for me. While we ate he complained about his contract negotiations with the Mets.

In the winter, we talked at the Greenwich YMCA, where we played merciless one-on-one basketball games against each other. Talk is not the right word. We cursed each other, mostly, as we hacked each other's arms, elbowed each other in the jaw, tried to trip each other on a drive to the basket. Those were vicious games, two big guys banging away at each other. Tom was graceless, and not a very good shooter. His best

9

move was to back me toward the basket and then go up for a little jump shot, clipping me on the jaw on his way up. I was a great shooter. I frustrated him with my long, uncontested jump shots, swish! His face got red. So I let him win. Not all the games. Only the last, deciding game. What the hell? He was Tom Seaver! He denied I ever let him win any of those games.

"You never let anyone win at anything in your life, Jordan," he said.

"I let you win, Tom. You're Tom Seaver, a big fucking star."

We talked, too, at Shea Stadium in his locker room after he pitched. Tom would be standing in front of a crowd of reporters, answering questions in his sweat-soaked uniform after yet another three-hit shutout. "Why did Pete Rose hit that fastball off the wall?" asked one reporter. Tom gave a nice, thoughtful answer about how he got the pitch up too much, where Rose could tomahawk it. Then, after the reporters left and he was sitting by his locker with me, he'd say in his shrill, girlish voice, "Do you believe that fucking question? I give up three fucking hits and all they want to talk about is Rose's double. Why not ask me about my twelve fucking strikeouts?"

Mostly, though, we talked over the phone. I'd call him the day after he had pitched a game I'd watched on television.

"Tom, it's me."

"What?"

"I saw you pitch last night." Silence. "Tom, you're not throwing enough curveballs."

"You think so?"

"Absolutely."

"Really?"

"Yep."

"What the fuck do you know?"

Like Tom, I had been a professional pitcher. We were a lot alike as pitchers. We were both six foot one, 200 pounds. We were both right-handers. We both had classic overhand deliveries. We both had great fastballs. Mine was faster, however. Tom won't admit that, but I suspect he knows it's true. That's why he can be caustic to me at times. Repressed envy. He figures, How can I admit such a fact? It would be embarrassing! He pitched in the major leagues for twenty years, then was elected, almost unanimously, to the Hall of Fame. I pitched in the minor leagues for three years of diminishing success, then outright failure before I was retired, forcibly, and returned to Connecticut to embark on my new career, digging ditches for a construction crew. Still, he insists on maintaining this fantasy that he had a better fastball than me. I indulge this fantasy now that we are both in our sixties. That's why I didn't mention our respective fastballs at first, when I called him recently to ask for a favor.

"Tom, it's me."

"What do you want?"

"Are you busy?"

"I'm working." It was four o'clock in the afternoon in Northern California, during a cold spell. There was the possibility of frost. "I'm putting my babies to sleep for the night," he said.

"You have more kids?"

"My grapes."

"Your grapes?"

"They're my babies."

"Jesus, Tom. You gotta get a life."

"You mean like yours? Spending all your days in an empty room? Staring at a blank piece of paper in a typewriter?" He laughed. "You call that a life?"

"You talk to grapes, for Chrissakes."

"I told you. They're my babies."

"Do they talk back?"

"What do you want?"

"I need a favor."

"What?"

I told him a story. My daughter hadn't spoken to me in twenty years because of the divorce. That's how kids see it when their parents divorce. "The Divorce." As if it's the only one. To them, it is, the only one that matters.

"So now, my grandson I've never met is asking about me," I told Tom. "He's eight, and he loves baseball. He wants to know his grandfather who was a baseball player. My daughter dropped me a note to tell me this."

"So, what can I do?"

"My daughter said it would mean a lot to my grandson if I could get him a baseball player's autograph. I told her I don't know any baseball players anymore. I haven't been in the clubhouse in years."

"Me too," said Tom. "Been there, done that."

"Then I thought of you."

"Send me his name and address, and I'll send him something."

"I'll e-mail it."

"I don't have e-mail."

"Then I'll fax it."

"I don't have a fax."

"Jesus, what are you, a recluse?"

"What do you think I should be doing? Playing celebrity golf tournaments?"

"I hope not."

"I tend my grapes, play with my dogs, and don't leave home unless it's to visit my daughter."

"Me, too. I tell people I don't leave my house unless I get paid."

"Why should you?"

"I'd rather stay home with my wife and dogs. I have six."

"Wives?"

"Dogs. Actually, only four now. Two died over the past three years. That was rough. Rougher even than my parents' dying."

"Tell me about it." We talked some more, about our quiet lives now, our wives, our dogs, our homes, our pleasure in cooking, but nothing about baseball. Tom said, "That part's over." I asked him how Nancy was. "The same," he said. I remembered Nancy from years ago. Pretty, blond, with a sweet sarcasm that made Tom splutter at times. I remembered his dog too, a Lab type. His name was Slider. Slider's long gone now. I told Tom once, "You shoulda had a dog named Curveball. Maybe you woulda had a longer career." He said, seriously, "I never really could understand the concept of a curveball."

I told him I'd send him a note with my grandson's name and address. He said, "The minute it hits my desk, I'll have it in the mail the same day."

"I shudder to think how much I'm gonna owe you for this."

"I'll think of something."

I couldn't control myself. I said, "I promise never again to remind you that I threw harder than you."

"In your dreams."

When I got off the phone I wrote my grandson's name and address on a piece of paper, added a little note thanking Tom again, and stuck the note inside the cover of one of my books. I inscribed the book "To Tom, who is my idol, just as I am his." I thought he'd like that. Then I Fed-Exed it all to him.

A week later my phone rang. I heard the voice of a little boy. He said his name, first and last, and then added very importantly, "I'm your grandson." It sounded strange, "grandson," from a little boy I'd never seen. He thanked me for Tom's autograph. Tom had sent him a photo of himself in a Mets uniform, with a nice inscription, telling my grandson that he'd heard from his grandfather, Tom's friend, that he was a future Hall of Famer.

"Now I'm going to have to root for the Mets, not the Phillies, Grandpa." I forgot that he lived in Philadelphia.

"The Mets are a better team anyway," I said. Then I told him to get the photo laminated so it wouldn't rip.

He said, "Tom sent it already laminated."

When my grandson got off the phone, my daughter got on. She thanked me for the autograph. "He won't put it down," she said. "He's afraid if he leaves the house, someone will steal it." I laughed. She added, "John's going to get it framed." It took me a split second to realize that John was my son-in-law, whom I'd never met.

"Good," I said. "I'm glad it made him happy."

My daughter was silent for a moment, then she said, "He wants to see you. He's telling everyone he has a grandfather who used to play baseball."

"Well, come on down to Florida," I said.

"We'll see."

That same day I got a note from my grandson, in perfect printing, thanking me for the autograph from Tom. He signed it, "To Grandpa with love," and his name. I also got a note from Tom on Little League organization stationery that read, "Done!" I picked up the phone and called him.

"What do you want now?" he bellowed above the noise of traffic in the background.

"Where are you?"

"I'm on the highway driving to my daughter's house for Christmas. She's got rug rats now." I remembered his daughter's name was Sarah. She was a cute little blond kid when I knew her. Now she must be a grown woman near forty.

I told Tom how thrilled my grandson was with the autograph, how he was getting it framed to hang on the wall of his bedroom. He said, "I know. He sent me a thank-you note." That was nice of my daughter, I thought. One of the many things about her I did not know.

"Did you read my book yet?" I asked.

"The first page."

"I shoulda sent you a little yellow ruler."

"Fuck you."

"If you need me to explain some of the bigger words, feel free to call." Tom harrumphed loudly. I added, "Did you like the inscription?"

"That's the same inscription you put on the last book you sent me. Where's your fucking creativity?"

"No, it isn't."

"Yes, it is." We squabbled back and forth over the past. Finally I said, "You're just jealous because you're a washed-up old ballplayer and I'm a young writer." We both laughed at that one.

"Talk about frustrated," he said. "You've never gotten over that you're not me."

I could understand why he thought that. He probably remembered the time I drove him to Shea for a game in the early '70s. It was pouring as we drove on the Connecticut Thruway in my gold 1970 Corvette with the T-tops that leaked. Rain seeped through the T-tops onto Tom's head. He looked up and laughed. "It leaks."

"No shit!" I wiped off the fogged-up windshield with my hand.

"Put on the defroster."

I glared at him. "It doesn't work."

He laughed again. "Why don't you just buy a Porsche?"

"I'm not Tom Seaver."

"That's for sure."

See what I mean? Maybe he was right: I did envy him, but I couldn't admit that then, or now, thirty-three years later, so I said, "Why should that frustrate me? You should be frustrated. I threw harder than you." I had broken my promise already, in less than a week.

"You wish."

"Remember what Terry Tatta said?" He feigned ignorance of that day in spring training thirty years ago. Tom and I were standing behind a batting cage in St. Petersburg when Terry, an umpire, approached us. Terry had umpired against me in the minor leagues in 1960, but fifteen years later he didn't recognize me at first. He talked to Tom for a few minutes, glancing at me curiously, until finally Terry's face brightened. He said, "I know you. I umpired against you in the Midwest League in 1960." He turned to Tom and added, "Tom, you wish you could bring it like this guy could."

"*That* never happened!" said Tom.

"Yes, it did," I said. "You've just repressed it."

"That's why you're in the Hall of Fame," Tom said.

"I still threw harder than you."

"Yeah, and between you and me we won 311 major-league games."

"Exactly! I tell everyone that!"

After we hung up I felt bad that I'd embarrassed Tom by reminding him about my superior fastball. So to assuage his bruised ego, I sent him a note. I told him that when my wife and I were still going together in our early forties, we had a terrible argument one night. She stood across the room with a glass of vodka in her hand, and I faced her from across the room with a glass of bourbon in mine.

Finally, in a fit of justified rage, she threw her glass at me. It missed my face by inches. I fired back. My glass missed her by three feet. She gave me a small, cold smile. Oh, how cruel women can be sometimes! Still smiling, she said, "No wonder you never made the big leagues."

I sent Tom that note. He'd like that story.

Brooks Robinson
LAURA LIPPMAN

I magine a scene straight from a fairy tale. An old crone has taken on an impossible task. She bends over thick books and ancient runes, squinting at fine print, muttering to herself. The clock is ticking. Come daylight, she must emerge from this dim lair, her locked room— or, if you prefer more accuracy in your fairy tales, an excellent local coffeehouse with free wireless—and perform the alchemical magic of which she has airily boasted for years. There is no Rumpelstiltskin to shoulder her undertaking, no genie or fairy godmother to whisper the answer in her ear. She must execute this feat alone. But if she can find the answer, the reward will be great. The years will fall away and she will be young again, in the flush of youth.

You see, although this wizened hag has never taken a statistics course in her life, although her only claim to fame as a baseball aficionado is that she told her husband to draft the rookie Dustin Pedroia for his fantasy team, she is determined to demonstrate what every reference source insists cannot be proved: *Brooks Robinson was the greatest third baseman to play the game.* Not the greatest defensive player, a fact seldom in dispute, but the greatest third baseman of all time.

I truly believe in the superiority of Brooks Robinson, and it's not because I'm a homer, a Baltimore girl who bleeds black and orange. Brooks Robinson may be my favorite baseball player, but Paul O'Neill is second, a pairing about as unlikely as the chocolate chip/orange sherbet double scoops I used to get at Baskin Robbins on the Baltimore Pike in those long-ago summers when the Orioles casually rolled to winning season after winning season. Now I have a fifteen-year-old stepson who has no conscious memories of the Orioles in postseason play. His father, a Washington Senators fan, is of little use; he can't quite stoke his son's Orioles love because of his own divided loyalties. No, I am the one who has bestowed upon my stepson most of the vintage Orioles cards in his collection—Jim Palmer, Frank Robinson, Mark Belanger. (Always had a soft spot for the Blade.) Now those cards gather dust as his attention wanders toward music and girls, and I am left with one card, literally and figuratively. It is an outsize photo of Brooks at spring training in 1967, slightly poochy at the midsection, a palm tree in the background. Perhaps if I can do justice to Brooks, invoke the perfect incantation, I will conjure up the return of Oriole Magic, remove the splinter of ice from my stepson's heart—and put my beloved birds back in contention.

Conventional wisdom maintains that Mike Schmidt was the greatest third baseman because of his superior offensive stats. The temptation is to eliminate him with a quick cheap shot: *There's no crying in baseball!* That would be wrong. Brooks—everyone in Baltimore is on a first-name basis with the Vacuum Cleaner—wouldn't want me to make a case for him by mocking another player. Besides, most of the experts I consulted put George Brett ahead of Brooks, and others have Brooks in fourth place behind Eddie Matthews or even further back. No, I can't rely on numbers to make my case, although there are some impressive ones—most hits, most games, most seasons, most assists, most put-outs, most double plays of any third baseman.

But we all know what Mark Twain said about statistics, right? Raise your hand if you remember Twain's old saw about lies, damned lies, and statistics. Now use that hand to smack yourself in the forehead, because it turns out that Twain didn't coin the phrase. He attributed the line to Disraeli. Yet a researcher at the University of York found more than a half-dozen variations of the old saying, all predating Twain's remark and none of them by the British prime minister. Isn't that reason enough to rethink what we think we know—Schmidt was the greatest—and consider my postulate that the title belongs to Brooks?

The word *postulate* is chosen carefully; geometry was the one area of mathematics in which I excelled. A theorem would demand that I prove that Brooks was the greatest player, whereas a postulate requires that you accept this as a given. Do you doubt Euclid on the assertion that two points determine a line segment? Then how can you question the amazing geometry of Brooks, his ability to move through multiple planes in any direction, intersecting the trajectory of line drive after line drive?

Brooks, like a lot of quintessential Baltimoreans—Unitas, Poe, and, um, me—wasn't actually born here. A native of Little Rock, Arkansas, he was already considered an outstanding prospect by his senior year of high school. My friend Joe Wallace, something of an expert in all things Cooperstown, was kind enough to send me this scouting report on Brooks, which he used in putting together *The Baseball Anthology*. It was written by a former major leaguer named Lindsay Deal, *who happened to go to church with the Robinson family*. How many other future Hall of Famers had endorsements from fellow congregants? It's just so Brooks.

February 13, 1955

I am writing you in regard to a kid named Brooks Robinson.

I think he measures up to having a good chance in major league baseball. I think he is a natural third baseman although he has been playing both second and third. He will be 18 years old on May 18 and graduates from Little Rock Senior High School on May 27. He is 6 ft. 1 in. and weighs 175. His physique is outstanding for a boy this age. He bats right and throws right. He is no speed demon but neither is he a truck horse. I believe in a year or two he will be above the average in speed. He hit well over .400 last year in American Legion baseball, including all tournament games. At the tournament in Altus, Oklahoma, he was awarded the trophy for being the outstanding player. Brooks has a lot of power, baseball savvy, and is always cool when the chips are down. This boy is the best prospect I've seen since Billy Goodman came to Atlanta to play when I was playing there. That's the reason I'm contacting you. I thought you might be interested in him and able to make as good an offer as anyone else. Otherwise, I wouldn't have bothered you with it. . . .

After reading that letter, I find myself wishing that Lindsay Deal might cast his eye on the economy or the stock market.

Brooks began his professional career in York, Pennsylvania, in the old Piedmont League. He started at second, but his manager— "wisely," as Brooks's Web site graciously phrases it—recommended he move to third. On September 17, 1955, Brooks was put into the Orioles lineup as a replacement for another rookie sidelined by an injury. He went two for four against the Senators and drove in a key run in the eighth inning.

I knew none of this when my family moved to Baltimore in 1965. Truth be told, I didn't know that much about Brooks's life story until I began researching this piece. But in 1966, when the Orioles swept the Dodgers to win the World Series—*when Brooks Robinson hit a home run off Don Drysdale in his first World Series at bat*—I became a fan. A fan who didn't really understand the game's intricacies, a fan who wouldn't learn how to keep score until well into my thirties, but a fan nonetheless. How coldhearted would a child have to be to resist the glory that was the Orioles in the 1960s and into the '70s? It was not only the era of the Oriole Way but of Earl Weaver and his tomatoes, Boog Powell, Frank Robinson, the legendary pitching staff of 1971. Years later, asked by a friend if I knew the history of the Baltimore Four, I replied in all seriousness, "Do you mean Palmer, McNally, Cuellar, and Dobson, during the season they all won twenty games or more?" It turns out that my friend was referring to a seminal draft board protest that predated the Catonsville Nine, but I maintain most Baltimoreans would answer as I did.

Brooks retired from baseball in 1977, the year I graduated from high school. (Hey, I told you I was a wizened crone.) In 1983, he was inducted into the Hall of Fame and the Orioles won, as of this writing, their last World Series championship. Living in exile in Texas, I entered into the lean years that test a fan's true mettle. In 1988, the Orioles established a record for consecutive losses, going 0–21 at the season's start and finishing in a distant, distant last place in the American League East, 54–107.

But in 1989, the year I was lucky enough to return to my beloved hometown, the Orioles staged a comeback that I couldn't help feeling was just for me. One of the key players was a local guy, Dave Johnson, a journeyman pitcher having the season of his life. "You're the Dave Johnson of journalism," my father said when I landed a job at the *Evening Sun*. The comparison was apt, and there was much to love about Johnson, not to mention manager Frank Robinson, Cal Ripken Jr., Mickey Tettleton, Pete Harnisch, Steve Finley, Curt Schilling, and even one of my old high school friends, Jim Traber. But Brooks remained my favorite Oriole. Wherever I lived, even during my first marriage, to a Yankees fan, I kept that Brooks card on my desk to remind myself that it was nice to be lucky, but it was luckier to be nice.

Niceness is a hard quality to measure, but I have to think that Brooks would be in contention as one of the nicest men in Cooperstown. How nice is Brooks Robinson? Brooks is so nice that he lent a rabid fan his uniform for Halloween 1975. Imagine another ballplayer, past or present, honoring such a request from a stranger. Brooks is so nice that he wooed his wife, a flight attendant on the team plane, by ordering endless glasses of *iced tea*. Brooks is so nice that he inspired an eponymous bluegrass song, which has the delightful refrain: "Brooooooooooooooooks Robinson/Old Reliable Number Five/They called him the Hoover/ He never let a ball get by." Brooks is so nice that when confronted by a blushing, babbling fan, he cheerfully consented to autograph a book. Actually, her book, written by her.

That was my Brooks moment, my only face-to-face meeting. I had gone to a favorite local bar, the Brass Elephant, to meet a former coworker. I am ashamed to tell you that he was the one who first recognized Brooks. But I am not ashamed to admit that I went complete and total fangirl. Now, I was a reporter for twenty years. I met presidential candidates and actors and musicians. I interviewed many of my literary heroes. But no encounter has affected me quite the same way as that brief moment with Brooks.

I was carrying a galley of my soon-to-be-published novel, my eighth. I had taken the plunge, quit my newspaper job, and a lot was riding on this book. I thrust it toward Brooks, who was enjoying a night out with his wife and another couple, and asked for the only autograph I have ever sought in my life. He cheerfully obliged:

"Laura—My best. Thanks for your support. See you, Brooks Robinson."

Every now and then, as I'm organizing my office, I check to make sure that I haven't given that particular book away by accident. I am careless with my own books. Despite advice, I have let first printings of my early works disappear, failed time and time again to invest in my own stock, only to watch the value of those relatively rare editions soar on the Internet. But the Brooks-autographed copy of *Every Secret Thing* is always there, a double talisman.

Brooks Robinson, like most of the players of his era, didn't know the kind of riches that today's players take for granted. His post-Orioles life has been full of various enterprises, from Crown Oil to chardonnay. But I have never met anyone in Baltimore who has a bad word to say about him, and it's a small town at heart. Act like an oaf, word gets around. Brooks may really be that rare person who doesn't have a mean bone in his body. As the song says:

> As the century nears the end, everybody's got a list
> The fans and the writers make their greatest pick
> Some say Brooks is second to Mike Schmidt
> To an Orioles fan, Mike Schmidt ain't
> BROOOOOOOOOOOOOOOOOOOOOOOOOOOOOOOOOOKS
> ROBINSON

You see? Even his song is nice. That's our Brooks.

My stepson is probably destined to be relatively indifferent to baseball for another decade or so; as I type these very words, he is burning through yet another guitar riff for, oh, about the 2,632nd time today. Still, there must be something that can bring him back into the fold. Perhaps a son of his own, or an Orioles season above .500. (He's only fifteen, so I really hope the latter comes along before the former.) He is old enough to remember Cal Ripken Jr.'s record and even went to Cooperstown to see him inducted, which was more than I was willing to do. Yes, maybe the Iron Man can drag him back, just as the Hoover grabbed hold of my loyalty and never let it go.

Lou Gehrig
JONATHAN EIG

I was raised in suburban New York in the 1970s, a seminormal, semiathletic, totally baseball-loving American boy. I played baseball board games—All-Star Baseball, *Sports Illustrated* Baseball, and Strat-O-Matic being my favorites. I played stickball. I played Little League. I played Wiffle ball. I collected baseball cards, and—for a few years, anyway—I probably knew the name of every starting player on every roster. Any time a major leaguer of even the smallest consequence came within a twenty-mile radius of my home to sign autographs at a car dealership or shopping mall, I was there.

Willie Mays used to make regular appearances during his sad, sluggish years with the Mets. I remember seeing him once at the finish line after a walk-a-thon to raise money for juvenile diabetes. He was dressed all in polyester—including a pair of pants that no shirt on earth could have possibly matched—and he yawned as if he couldn't wait to make a basket catch of his appearance check and get the hell out of there. Still, it was one of the great moments of my young life.

Ron Blomberg, baseball's first designated hitter and a double hero in my book for having been born Jewish, came to my summer camp one year. He wore very short terry-cloth tennis shorts and sandals. He gave the kids some tips on hitting and let us each pose for a picture standing by his side. His Louisville Slugger, which I got to hold when the picture was snapped, tilted in my arms like a telephone pole. This moment thrilled me even more than the encounter with Mays for the simple reason that Blomberg was a Yankee.

The player I most longed to meet was Bobby Murcer, the graceful center fielder who had come along in 1965, the year after I was born, and made the All-Star team for the first time in 1971, just as I was becoming fully aware of baseball and enamored of the Yanks. I cried like a five-year-old—I was eleven—when they traded him in 1975. Years later, in my early twenties, I was working on a profile of Phil Rizzuto for a newspaper when I spotted Murcer strolling near the Yankees broadcast booth. I tried to greet him, but the words came out all wrong and I broke out in a drenching sweat. I apologized and walked away.

I'd still go to games. I'd still read the sports section of my newspaper first, starting with the box scores. But idol worship steadily ran its course, and by the summer of 2001, with the chemically enlarged Barry Bonds making a mockery of the record books, eventually belting seventy-three home runs, my view of the baseball hero as a species had spun 180 degrees. When I was a boy, only the action on the field had mattered. Now that I was an adult, I was all too aware of the game's off-field realities: the ego trips, labor disputes, drug scandals, and contract squabbles. As a boy, I hadn't cared a bit if my heroes were decent or dreadful people. They were ballplayers, and that was all. Now, with Bonds, one of the greatest ballplayers of all time struck me as one of lowest pieces of dung ever scraped from the bottom of a shoe. He didn't just kill the notion of ballplayer as hero. He beat it to a bloody, lifeless pulp, and stood over the corpse and sneered.

That summer I happened to be reading Laura Hillenbrand's marvelous book *Seabiscuit,* which had just hit stores and was not yet a nationwide phenomenon and mega best-seller. I fell in love with it from the first paragraph: "In 1938, near the end of a decade of monumental turmoil, the year's number-one newsmaker was not Franklin Delano Roosevelt, Hitler, or Mussolini. It wasn't Pope Pius XI, nor was it Lou Gehrig, Howard Hughes, or Clark Gable. The subject of the most newspaper column inches in 1938 wasn't even a person. It was an undersized, crooked-legged racehorse named Seabiscuit."

I thought Gehrig seemed like an odd fit for that paragraph. Was he ever a celebrity of the same magnitude as Howard Hughes or Clark Gable? I doubted it. He was a marvelous ballplayer, of course; the greatest first baseman the game had ever seen. But had he ever been beloved by Americans the way Babe Ruth or even Christy Mathewson had? It seemed improbable. Certainly, I had never felt any great excitement for Lou, who had always struck me as boringly efficient on the field and hopelessly stiff off it. But Hillenbrand's curious inclusion stuck with me.

One night that summer, my wife and I were having dinner in our little apartment by the lake in Chicago. I was telling her how much I was enjoying *Seabiscuit*, and how Hillenbrand made me feel about this horse the way I felt about some of my baseball heroes growing up. I was rooting passionately. I was investing my emotions in contests that had no impact on my life whatsoever. And it wasn't even that I cared about the competition or even really understood the intricacies of horse racing. It was the context, not the contest, that made the story riveting. Hillenbrand made me see the crowds and smell the cigar smoke. She made me understand why an overmatched horse might captivate the nation when so many were struggling through the Depression.

At one point in my rambling, I mentioned Gehrig.

"Some writer could do the same sort of thing with him," I told my wife. "His story isn't really about baseball. Nobody ever says Lou Gehrig is his favorite player of all time. Nobody can recall a single moment on the field in which he made history. He was one of the greatest baseball players who ever played, but he hardly ever did anything dramatic. Sure, he played in 2,130 consecutive games. But that's like assembling the world's largest collection of wine corks or something. Sure, it's impressive when you get done, but it's boring as hell along the way. And then, when he's still in his midthirties, the guy finds out he's dying."

I was in my midthirties. I stopped and thought about it. When I looked up, I could see that my wife was nodding her head in the way she sometimes does when I go on too long about baseball.

"That's the story!" I exclaimed. "An athlete struck down in his prime by an incurable disease. What was that like? How did he handle it? How the hell did the most boring guy in the history of the game make such a remarkable speech? Why did he call himself the luckiest man? Somebody ought to write *that* book. The baseball would be the background. The action on the field would be the buildup to the moment he gets sick. That's the way the story ought to be told."

"So," she said, "why don't you do it?"

I spent the next three years researching every detail of Gehrig's life. I walked the streets of the New York City neighborhood where he grew up, the only surviving child of poor German immigrants. I spent countless hours in libraries looking at old photos of New York in the 1900s. I went through microfilm reels trying to figure out how and when his baby sisters and brothers died. I paged through old newspapers watching Gehrig develop into a promising high school athlete and then a college star. I followed him, game by game, box score by box score, as he broke in with the Yankees and began hitting enough home runs to become a star of the first order. I interviewed dozens of people who had known Gehrig or had seen him play.

But who was this shy man who was consuming so much of my time and attention? I knew his tendencies as a batter—he was such a disciplined hitter and so adept at hitting line drives, for example, that he never learned to pull the ball and aim for Yankee Stadium's short right-field porch, which is why he usually led the team in triples and not home runs. But his personality eluded me. I worried that my book would have no soul, that Gehrig would crumble and slide from the pages like dried leaves. I tried to remind myself that Hillenbrand wrote a terrific book about a sports hero who couldn't talk. Surely, Gehrig's personality had to be more interesting than Seabiscuit's. But I had my doubts. One night I dreamed that I was driving an old Model T when, up ahead on the side of the road, I spotted Gehrig and Ruth standing by a wooden fence, as if waiting for a ride. I stopped the car, got out, and tried to talk to Gehrig, but he laughed and turned away.

I wrote my book chronologically, researching and writing his childhood first, and then his career with the Yankees. He gave a few interviews at the height of his career, but not as many as I would have liked. He was painfully shy. He liked talking about baseball but not about himself. I unearthed a few interesting details. I found evidence of an old girlfriend, a beautiful college girl from Westchester, and discovered that Lou's mother had broken up the relationship. Gehrig, a Hall of Fame mama's boy, never complained.

I learned that Gehrig was a great lover of dogs and owned a pure-bred German shepherd that he entered in kennel club shows. I learned he was famously cheap. I learned that he loved his teammates and would invite them to come and stay with his mother and father when they were homesick or ill or slumping, but that he still never felt like one of the boys.

Only when he met and married Eleanor Twitchell did he begin to come into his own. Even then, it wasn't easy. Gehrig was one of the handsomest men in baseball, but he seemed unsure of himself in pursuing his bride. Eleanor, a former flapper, was his opposite in most ways. She smoked and drank and gambled and, by some accounts, slept around a bit—perhaps even with Ruth. But Lou and Eleanor loved each other, and who's to say what makes a marriage work? This one did.

Eleanor taught her husband to stop sneaking in and out of Yankee Stadium. Take your time and sign autographs for the kids, she urged him. She taught him to fight the team for more money. It had always been Gehrig's habit to gratefully accept whatever salary the Yanks thought he deserved. Somehow, she even persuaded him to go to Hollywood and audition for the movies. In his lone motion picture, a cowboy musical called *Rawhide,* one can see his discomfort in every frame of film, but one can also see the little boy in him, thrilled at the chance to ride horses and fire six-guns.

Step by step, I was beginning to figure him out. Or I thought I was, anyway. He struck me as smart, sensitive, and insecure: a decent man who loved the game but was never comfortable with his celebrity. But I still wasn't sure. I still sensed I was merely scratching the surface.

One day, while digging through a massive stack of baseball memorabilia auction catalogues, looking for items connected to Gehrig, I came across a collection of letters he had written to his doctor over the final years of his life. Gehrig kept no diaries. He never wrote an autobiography. He and Eleanor never had any children. His medical records were permanently sealed. It was as if he'd disappeared without a trace. But now, with these letters, I had a chance to see the real, unfiltered Gehrig. I was desperate to get my hands on them.

Shortly after he made his movie, in the spring of 1938, Gehrig went to spring training with the rest of the Yankees. Almost immediately, he began to complain of cramps in his legs and blisters on his hands. He had trouble making solid contact even on batting-practice pitches. Some said the bright lights of Hollywood had damaged his eyes. Others said his consecutive-game streak had finally caught up with him.

That's when he did something he'd never done before: He sat out a game to rest his aching body. It was only a spring training game, but it broke his heart nonetheless.

As the season wore on, he grew more and more confused. Clearly, something was wrong with his body, but he didn't have any idea what it was. So he fought through it. He began ordering lighter bats. He tinkered with his batting stance. He stepped up his exercise routine.

He expressed frustration, but he never made excuses.

He finished the season with a .295 average, 28 home runs and 114 RBIs. Oh, and he helped the Yankees win another World Series, their sixth championship in his fourteenth full season. Given what we know now about his health, Gehrig's performance in 1938 might qualify as the most amazing individual feat in the history of the game. But when the season was over, he was so disappointed with himself that, for the first time anyone could remember, he went out and got plastered.

The next season, he showed up for spring training looking like a different man. His shoulders and elbows poked at his sleeves as if he were a scarecrow, all stick and straw. His hair had gone gray, his face gaunt. He still had no idea he was sick, although he knew beyond a doubt that something was terribly amiss.

Finally, in early June, he pulled himself out of the lineup and went to the Mayo Clinic, where he was diagnosed with Amyotrophic Lateral Sclerosis, the disease that would kill him two years later. But before he disappeared from the public eye, he reluctantly agreed to speak to the fans who showed up in his honor on July 4, 1939, at Yankee Stadium. That's when he made his gut-wrenching speech, saying that he wasn't going to be defined by his illness, that he was going to be defined by his life, that he was "the luckiest man on the face of the earth" to have been blessed with so much good fortune.

After his speech was when he began writing to his doctor at the Mayo Clinic, documenting his physical and emotional condition in heartbreaking and at times gruesome detail. It took me six months to locate those letters, in the hands of an autograph collector in Maryland and seen by no more than two or three people in the world. As I awaited delivery, I worried. These were Gehrig's private papers. He had no reason to believe anyone would come along and scrutinize them sixty years later. What if they revealed he wasn't the strong and decent man I thought? What if he had moped and whined? What if he had cursed God? What if, in frustration, he admitted that he had mistreated his wife? What if he confessed to using steroids throughout his career? OK, this last one was unlikely, given that they hadn't been invented yet. But still, my mind reeled at the possibilities.

When I finally received them, I was so nervous I could barely hold the pages. By the time I finished reading, I could barely keep from crying. Gehrig proved to be everything I thought he was and more. He handled his illness with grace and good humor. He searched desperately for a cure, for a way out of his predicament. But when he saw that he had no chance, he accepted his fate with the greatest courage I have ever known.

"Don't think that I am depressed or pessimistic," he wrote just months before his death. "I intend to hold on as long as possible and then if the inevitable comes, I will accept it philosophically and hope for the best. That's all we can do."

When I was a boy, baseball was all about fantasy. Beginning with Ron Blomberg's shorts and Mays's polyester pants, the fantasy began to fade. Reality slowly settled in. And reality was not as much fun. But with Gehrig, I never had to cling to my childish ideas of what it meant to be a hero. He never wanted to be famous. All he wanted to do was play ball and take care of his family. The true depth of his character became clear when things didn't work out the way he had planned.

That's what makes him a hero for any age.

Pedro Martinez
SETH MNOOKIN

One of the joys of baseball is arguing about the answers to the sport's ever-debatable questions. Is Ty Cobb the nastiest man in the Hall of Fame? Will anybody ever convince Joe Morgan that Billy Beane did not write *Moneyball*? Is Derek Jeter the worst fielding shortstop ever to win a Gold Glove?

For the absolutists out there, there are a handful of things that are not in dispute. Like: Babe Ruth is the best player in the history of the game. No single moment will ever encapsulate a player better than Ted Williams's career-ending, crowd-spiting home run did. Dock Ellis is the only person who will ever throw a no-hitter on acid.*

---

* Ellis, one of the great forgotten characters of baseball, threw his Electric Kool-Aid No-No on June 12, 1970. Describing that day, he said, "There were times when the ball was hit back at me. I jumped because I thought it was coming fast but the ball was coming slow. . . . I covered first base and I caught the ball and I tagged the base all in one motion and I said, 'Ooh, I just made a touchdown.'" Another great Ellis anecdote: On May 1, 1974, he accused his teammates of going soft. "We gonna get down," he said before taking the mound against the Cincinnati Reds that day. "We gonna do the do. I'm going to hit these motherfuckers." True to his word, Ellis hit Pete Rose, Joe Morgan, and Dan Driessen to start the game. After walking Tony Perez, Ellis threw two pitches at Johnny Bench's head—and *still* wasn't thrown out of the game. It was the '70s.

And, of course: Nobody has ever had a two-year stretch as brilliant, as dominating, as absolutely *electrifying* as Pedro Martinez's 1999 and 2000 seasons with the Boston Red Sox. Lefty Grove's 1930 and 1931 campaigns? Please. Bob Gibson in '68 and '69? Not even close. Mid-'90s Greg Maddux? Actually, Maddux gives Pedro a run for his money . . . but ultimately loses out on style points. Maddux wore starched jeans; Pedro embroidered Linus (of the comic strip *Peanuts*) patches on his ass and sported Jheri Curls. Maddux said things like, "I could probably throw harder if I wanted, but why?" Pedro countered with, "Wake up the damn Bambino and have me face him. Maybe I'll drill him in the ass." Maddux frustrated hitters; Pedro made them look foolish.

> *In-between days, part one: August 27, 1998. With his teammates on the field, Pedro wanders into the dugout in the middle of the first inning of a game against Oakland wearing a rubber Yoda mask and 220-pound reliever Jim Corsi's uniform top. Pedro later denied having anything to do with the incident. "I'm not that ugly," he said. "Corsi is."*

Let's start with 1999: There's the gaudy 23–4 record, the supermodel-thin 2.07 ERA, the 13.2 strikeouts per nine innings, the fact that he gave up only nine home runs at the height of the steroids era, the absolutely *ridiculous* .923 walks-plus-hits per inning pitched. There's Pedro's pitching line at the All-Star Game at Fenway Park. He faced six batters, four of whom had won MVP awards. He struck out five . . . including the first four in a row. There's his playoff record: 2–0, seventeen innings pitched, twenty-three Ks, and a 0.00 ERA.

But numbers don't capture what it was like to watch him on the mound. Generously listed at five foot eleven and 175 pounds, he had, as a *Sports Illustrated* cover story put it, "the body of Bud Selig"—and yet in action he looked more like a matador. He'd rock back in the middle of his windup, almost as if he wanted to savor those last moments before throwing home, and then he'd bring his arm—the right arm of God—behind his head and twist his glove back toward his body. His baby face would go hard; his lips would curl down in a sneer; he'd whip around toward the plate; and then he'd hop a little at the end, a punctuation mark accenting perfection. No matter what he was throwing— his tailing, upper-nineties fastball; his low-eighties, Bugs Bunny change; his knee-buckling, holy-shit curve—his arm angle remained the same, leaving hitters blindly flailing away. No one—not Randy Johnson, not Mariano Rivera, not Roger Clemens—made so many great hitters look so bad so often.

> *In-between days, part two: June 25, 1999. Three of Pedro's teammates tape him to a pole in the Red Sox dugout during a game against the White Sox. They leave him there, with his mouth sealed shut, as the players congratulate one another on the field after the game. Later, Pedro tells the media, "They said I was moving around too much, I guess. They're crazy, those guys."*

Every game Pedro pitched in 1999 was an Event; even so, a couple stand out. The season's first spine-tingling moment came on June 4, when he squared off against Tom Glavine, the Braves' reigning Cy Young Award winner. Pedro fanned Brian Jordan to end the first, Gerald Williams to finish off the second, Chipper Jones to complete the third, and Ryan Klesko to close out the fourth. By the middle of the game, the Boston crowd seemed to be possessed; when Derek Lowe stood up in the Sox's bullpen in the top of the seventh to throw a side session, he was booed so loudly he couldn't hear himself speak. Pedro notched sixteen strikeouts that day. All fifty-seven of his fastballs clocked in at ninety-four miles per hour or higher; forty-two of them were strikes.

When asked about what it was like in Fenway that afternoon, Braves manager Bobby Cox said, "This was different than in the Metrodome in the '91 World Series"—when the crowd was recorded at 125 decibels, comparable to a jet airliner. "That was pure noise. This was a celebration." Hall of Fame sportswriter Peter Gammons was equally awestruck. "It was never quite the same way when Roger Clemens pitched," he wrote in an article for *ESPN: The Magazine*. "There was an electricity to the way he grunted and charged the mound in his halcyon Fenway days, but he didn't touch the soul of Fenway people."* Perhaps Sox catcher Jason Varitek summed it up best: "Once every five days, New England becomes Pedro's world. The rest of us just work here."

> *In-between days, part three: April 24, 2000. With Pedro's brother Ramon Martinez on the mound, Rangers designated hitter David Segui takes ball four. In the Sox's dugout, Pedro sticks his thumbs under his armpits and begins squawking like a chicken. "Come on, Segui! Swing the bat!" Segui reportedly is none too amused.*

Even more memorable was Friday, September 10, the first night of a three-game series at Yankee Stadium. Pedro hit Chuck Knoblauch to lead off the game, and six batters later Chili Davis went deep to give New York a 1–0 lead. But after that it was lights out, as Pedro sat down

---

* Pedro versus Roger, pt. 1: On April 29, 1986, Clemens set a major-league record when he struck out twenty Seattle Mariners. That year, the Mariners had the most strikeouts and the worst record in the American League. On September 18, 1996, Clemens tied his own record while pitching against Detroit. The '96 Tigers had the most strikeouts and the worst record in baseball. In comparison, the 1999 Braves ended the year with 103 wins—the most in either league—while the Yankees, the second-best-hitting team in the AL, were in the middle of a run in which they'd win three out of four World Series.

the last twenty-two batters he faced. When it was all over, he'd struck out seventeen hitters, including the last five of the game. Still more incredible, he walked off the mound with tens of thousands of Yankees fans chanting his name. Nothing so perfectly captures the magic of that mystical season as the fact that for one night, the upper deck at Yankee Stadium was decorated with giant "K" signs *for a Red Sox pitcher*.

That night in the clubhouse, Yankees' manager Joe Torre—who played with Gibson and Tom Seaver at their peaks and faced Sandy Koufax and Steve Carlton in their primes—said, "That was as close to unhittable as you can find." Red Sox manager Jimy Williams, who was a coach with Atlanta when Braves pitchers won six straight Cy Youngs, said, "I've never seen anyone pitch like he did tonight." And Yankees' pitcher David Cone, less than two months removed from recording the sixteenth perfect game in Major League history, said it was the best-pitched game he'd ever seen.

> *In-between days, part four: Summer 2001. Pedro agrees to do a quick Q&A for Sports Illustrated for Kids. Favorite color? "Green." Favorite book? "Whatever." Favorite actress? "Sandra Bullock." Secret ambition? "I would like to fuck Sandra Bullock." When asked to give an answer that was more appropriate for a children's magazine, Pedro replied, "I would like to sleep with Sandra Bullock."*

The cherry on the top of '99 came Monday, October 11. Five days earlier, Pedro had left the opening game of the Red Sox's best-of-five playoff series against the Cleveland Indians with a strained muscle in his back. After losing that game and the next, the Sox had improbably fought back to force an all-in Game Five at Jacobs Field. Before the game, Williams had said there was no way he was going to let Pedro take the mound that night: "We can't hurt the kid." Pedro, however, thought differently, and after watching his teammates cough up leads of 2–0 and 7–5 in the first three innings, he came out to start the fourth. Two days earlier, his injured back and shoulder had caused him to fight back tears. He couldn't raise his arm high enough to throw from his normal slot, and his fastball didn't break ninety miles per hour. And still, he no-hit the hard-slugging Indians* for six innings, finessing eight strikeouts on guile and guts rather than brute force.

A week later, the Sox's season was done: They lost to the Yankees, four games to one, in the American League Championship Series. The sole Red Sox victory came in Game Three, when Pedro annihilated Clemens and the Yankees 13–1—the game that prompted the famous Fenway chant: "Where is Roger?" "In the shower!"† It was the only playoff game the Yankees would lose all year.

> *In-between days, part five: August 2004. Orlando Cabrera arrives in the Boston clubhouse after being brought on to replace Red Sox icon Nomar Garciaparra, who'd been traded to the Chicago Cubs. Pedro presents the team's new shortstop with a "Stop Smoking" poster he'd posed for several years earlier. It was, of course, personally inscribed: "I'm a flamin' mullion with a big pecker and a big bank account. Pedro Martinez, #45."*

The 1999 season was the type old men tell their grandchildren about . . . and still, it wasn't as impressive as Pedro's 2000 campaign. His 18–6 record should have been even better: He got two losses and one no-decision in games in which he gave up two runs or less. He

---

* Just how hard-slugging, you ask? Well, the Indians' outfield had an aggregate on-base percentage of .420. They led the league in runs-per-game and all of baseball with a .372 OBP. They were the first team since 1950 to score more than 1,000 runs in a season. You get the idea.

† Pedro versus Roger, pt. 2: In his nine playoff games with the Red Sox, Clemens went 1–2. In his thirteen games, Pedro went 6–2.

brought his ERA down another third of a run, to 1.74—and this was when the league average was 4.92. (In comparison, when Koufax posted his 1.73 ERA in 1966, the league average was 3.61.*) He set an all-time record when he lowered his WHIP to .737. His K/BB rate was the third-best since 1900. I could go on.

There were no playoff starts that year, however, no epic perform-ances against the Yankees in the Bronx; in fact, the year's best game may very well have been a late August matchup with Tampa Bay that is best remembered for beanballs and brawls. Before that game, Pedro hadn't won in three starts against the Rays going back to 1999. He nailed Gerald Williams on the left hand with his fourth pitch, setting off the night's first of two bench-clearing melees. He then proceeded to sit down twenty-four batters in a row before giving up a single to lead off the ninth. It was one of four shutouts he'd throw that year.[†]

In-between days, part six: September 28, 2004. Pedro brings twenty-eight-inch Dominican dwarf Nelson de la Rosa to the Red Sox club-

---

* Fun with numbers: If the 2000 edition of Pedro had pitched in 1966, he would have had an ERA of 1.28, which is 35 percent lower than Koufax's—not percentage points, *percent*. His ERA in his six losses—2.44—would *still* have been the league's overall best by more than a run. Pedro's 2000 ERA was 183 percent lower than the league average; if a hitter had a batting average 183 percent higher than the league average, he'd have hit .773. And his 2000 ERA+ of 291 is better than anything Koufax or Grove or Walter Johnson put up; in fact, it's better than everyone except for Tim Keefe, who set the all-time record of 294 . . . in 1880.

[†] No pitcher has ever come closer to pitching a perfect game without ac-tually pitching one: On June 3, 1995, Pedro threw nine perfect innings while pitching for the Montreal Expos against the San Diego Padres. The Expos fi-nally scored a run in the top of the tenth. In the bottom of the tenth, Padres left fielder Bip Roberts led off with a double. Pedro got credit for the win, but his twenty-seven consecutive outs to begin the game don't count as either a perfect game or a no-hitter.

house. "He's a very funny character, and very animated," Pedro explains. "Everybody's happy with him. He's our good luck charm."

As hard as it is to believe, Pedro's career in Boston did not start all that well. Over a series of four starts beginning in late May 1998, he gave up almost a run per inning. He was booed at Fenway. He began to brood. He lost weight. Eventually, he was diagnosed with gastritis, a swelling of the stomach walls caused by stress. He was, to put it bluntly, suffering from insecurity.

And that may be Pedro's most appealing characteristic of all. For all the bravado and swagger, he has always acted as if his time was limited and he had something to prove. At the end of his '99 campaign, he took some totally gratuitous—and totally typical—swipes at the Dodgers, who half a decade earlier had traded him to Montreal because they didn't think he was durable enough to be a starting pitcher. "I'm a living example of the mistakes the Dodgers have made," he said. "I'm glad . . . the Dodgers are back home watching on TV."

Pedro's command is legendary—his walks-per-inning ratio is, not surprisingly, among the best ever—but he was often near the league leaders in hit batsmen. This was not, I'm convinced, because he was a headhunter: It was because he had to remind himself that despite weighing less than many high school seniors, he really could still strike fear in the hearts of opposing batters.* Every time Pedro took the mound, he knew—we all knew—that his body and his brilliance

---

* It's no coincidence that he led off that '99 game in New York and '00 game in Tampa by hitting a batter. And during the infamous October 11, 2003, playoff start against the Yankees—the game where he ended up flinging Don Zimmer to the ground—Pedro gave up a walk, a single, and a double to lead off the fourth inning and then hit utility outfielder Karim Garcia with his next pitch. Before that, he'd given up six hits and four earned runs. In his four remaining innings, not a single Yankee reached base.

had an expiration date. And unlike Clemens, unlike Bonds, unlike Manny, we have watched Pedro age before our eyes. Part of what was so heartbreaking about the Red Sox's loss in Game Seven of the 2003 ALCS was that by the end of the seventh inning, Pedro clearly knew what Grady Little did not: The once-invincible gunslinger was out of bullets.

Pedro began the 2009 season as a thirty-seven-year-old unsigned free agent. It wasn't until July, when the World Champion Phillies' starting pitching broke down, that a team decided to take a chance on the most dominant pitcher in the history of the game. As of this writing, his $1 million deal looks like the bargain basement steal of the year: After seven starts, he's 5–0 with a 2.87 ERA.

Last night he pitched against the Mets, the team he signed with and, because of an injury, for whom he performed underwhelmingly after leaving the Red Sox in 2004. I turned off the TV after his twenty-pitch first inning, when he gave up a line-drive single to Luis Castillo to start the game and threw four straight balls to Carlos Beltran. This morning at breakfast, I almost didn't want to learn how the game turned out.

I shouldn't have worried: Pedro threw eight shutout innings in one of his most dominating starts of the year. His only real jam came in the second, when the Mets had Castillo at the plate and runners on second and third. Pedro drilled Castillo on his right arm to load the bases—and then proceeded to retire the next ten batters in a row.

Albert Pujols
BUZZ BISSINGER

I n the cloister of St. Louis they immediately knew the miracle of what they were seeing, but by their very nature were far too polite to brag and blather about it. This wasn't Boston or, God forbid, New York, where stripper sightings of Alex Rodriguez sent the tabloids into a slobber of salivation far more exciting than a steal of home. If word of the celestial presence never traveled further than the Gateway Arch and the mighty Mississippi, that was perfectly fine. Remember, they were St. Louisans, not starry-eyed shepherds.

It would take an outsider to spread the gospel, turn the arrogant skeptics into believers, not just in New York and Boston but in Philadelphia and Chicago and Los Angeles and San Francisco and even Milwaukee, *Milwaukee*. Somebody would have to step in, take credit even if no credit was due, because this is America, after all. So I have decided, much like Galileo would have done had he redirected his life to the study of something truly important, that I am the one who made the single greatest public discovery in the cosmology of baseball:

Albert.

Albert Pujols.

As I was writing the book *Three Nights in August,* in which I spent much of the 2003 season with manager Tony La Russa and the St. Louis Cardinals, I made a conscious decision to refer to Pujols as the Great Pujols. I had watched him play nearly fifty times that year, carefully observed him not simply at the plate, with that swing somehow both long and quick as a cat, but in the private interior of the clubhouse, where much of the real work of hitting takes place for those few willing to do it. The conclusion was obvious. He was the *Great* Pujols: *Great* because of that swing and sound off the bat, as if a huge tree branch had suddenly snapped; *Great* because of his ability to take walks when walks were needed; *Great* because of his instinctive aggressiveness on the base path even though he was slower than a septuagenarian looking for supermarket specials; *Great* because of a sweeping grace despite being six foot three and 230 pounds; *Great* because of his versatility in the field such that he had played every position for the Cardinals except catcher, center field, and pitcher.

I had no choice, even then in 2003, in only his third season. He had hit .359 that year to lead the National League. He also led the league in hits (212) and doubles (51). He had 43 home runs and 124 RBIs. He was the first player in major-league history to have at least 30 home runs and 100 RBIs in his first three seasons. All of this at the age of twenty-three.

Arguments over who was better were petty and annoying, flicks of lint off the lapel. But after the book was published, the finicky mosquitoes came out with their low-drone whines that I had overreached. The familiar names of Rodriguez and Barry Bonds were invoked with straight and serious faces. Some had the psychosis to mention the Colorado Rockies' Todd Helton or Manny Ramirez, then of the Red Sox. The Yankees' Derek Jeter was pulled out, because, like a favorite pair of slippers, he is always pulled out.

I held to my description. But the responses back always had a sub-text: He plays for St. Louis, a small-market team in the frumpy Midwest, so it doesn't really count.

It wasn't until October 4, 2004, as the Cardinals were on their way to the World Series, that Pujols for the first time appeared on the cover of *Sports Illustrated*. And the story wasn't about him but the team as a whole regardless of a season in which he batted .331, led the league in runs scored, hit 46 home runs and had 123 RBIs. Perhaps the most remarkable statistic was the number of times he had struck out—52 times in 592 at bats. Compare that with Mickey Mantle, who his fourth full season in the major leagues struck out 97 times. Or Rodriguez, who struck out 109 times in his fourth season. Or Bonds, back in the day when he wasn't looking like the inflatable Shrek in the Macy's Thanksgiving Day Parade, striking out 93 times.

Forget these players anyway. Pujols's statistical lines were far more comparable to such greats as Hank Aaron and Joe DiMaggio in the beginning of their careers. There were variations, of course. DiMaggio struck out far less than Pujols (an amazing twenty times) but also had appreciably fewer home runs. Aaron's statistical line his fourth season was similar, although Aaron not only had fewer home runs but an inferior on-base percentage, slugging average, and batting average.

Today, of course, everybody finally knows without dissension. *Sports Illustrated* put Pujols on the cover again in 2009, asserting without equivocation that he was a first ballot Hall of Famer. *USA Today* weighed in with a lengthy paean under the headline "Cardinals Slugger Albert Pujols Is Batting Cleanup for Baseball." Bill James, the relentless statistical guru who finds rot beneath every traditional measure, said that Pujols might be the most perfect player in baseball history based on being great from the start, his career uninterrupted by sustained injuries or wars with management, and posting a Hall of Fame season every year.

So he has finally arrived, no longer the secret of St. Louis. And yet. . . .

Because of the drug-induced taint of Rodriguez and Bonds and Ramirez and the swarm of suspicion over Roger Clemens and Mark McGwire, it is likely Pujols will forever play with an asterisk next to his name—*please be advised that this player may have used performance-enhancing substances.*

There is no proof, but because suspicion of illegal drug use is omnipresent thanks to the see-no-evil, speak-no-evil idiocy of baseball ownership and the players' union for years, no proof is necessary. The better Pujols gets, the more the media speculation—guilt by association all that's needed. He has insisted over and over that he has never taken any kind of performance-enhancing drug. I have seen Albert Pujols at work in a way that no writer has ever witnessed, and I believe him.

I believe him not only because of the way he plays baseball but because of the way he prepares for it in those wee clubhouse pregame hours, when most players stuff their pockets with sunflower seeds or use a specially designed machine to make sure their cap fits perfectly or duck into the dining area for a thorough study of the buffet line in the excited hope of a new-style omelette. I have watched him, still in his Cardinal red undergarments in a stiff-backed chair, scan hour after hour of video to find the infinitesimal giveaways that every pitcher has, no matter how great. I have watched him analyze his swing—too down on his legs, moving around too much, too busy at the plate—running the same sliver of video over and over, back and forth, back and forth, to the degree where tedium is a vast understatement.

He does a variation of the same during games, trundling off into the clubhouse after at bats, sitting side by side with Cardinal video coordinator Chad Payne to scrutinize what the pitcher is trying to do to him and how. If he is fooled once, he will never be twice, the holes sealed tight. One day in May 2003 he dissected his first at bat against the Expos' Claudio Vargas, a woeful three-pitch strikeout. He studied his hands and his stride in reaction to Vargas's delivery. He noted that he had three more at bats to get even, but it only took the next one—a 452-foot shot over the center field wall. Over and over he does what so few baseball players do with more than lip service: Use the bedrock of talent as only the first layer to get to somewhere else. For many players, a two-hit day is more than enough to justify their obscene millions. For Pujols, a two-hit day should be a three-hit day, a three-hit day a four-hit day, a four-hit day a five-hit day. On every at bat he undertakes what may be the single-hardest act in all of sports: relentless concentration.

But I also believe him because of the way he lives, far more exceptional than anything he has ever done at Busch or the overrated decrepitude of Wrigley, where leaks in pipes of the bowels are anything but cozy, or the urine stink of Shea before it was mercifully condemned. In the sanctity of the clubhouse empty of reporters, with no clinging posse encircling him like palace guards, he serves as big brother and mentor to younger players, Latino in particular. He listens to La Russa, drawing from him, never giving off the whiff of *nobody tells me how to play this game*. During interviews, he talks about his life not in the familiar rote of *I'm only talking to this writer because the club says I have to* but with singular grace and humility.

From virtually penniless roots in the Dominican Republic, where he lived for more than a decade, much of it in a makeshift campsite, he came to the United States in the 1990s and was raised by his grandmother. He talks about her with his head cocked in contrition, about how she moved the family to Missouri from New York after Albert saw a man get shot outside a grocery store as a teenager. When he took up baseball seriously, the naysayers said he could never make it because

he was too slow afoot and didn't pull the ball enough and wasn't suited
to any particular position and was the 402nd pick of the 1999 draft,
out of a community college nobody had ever heard of, and signed for
about $30,000. The early labors were hard, humiliating. But Pujols,
like all great athletes, possessed immutable self-confidence. He smiles
with bemusement when he talks about those days, the Great Pujols
considered at best the Mediocre Pujols. Then he talks about his family,
and there is a tidal wave of tonal shift.

All celebrities, sports or Hollywood or political, invoke their families as special. It is a time-honored tradition, even after getting a
farewell tongue bath from the girl from Argentina when they are supposedly studying the rock formations of the Appalachian Trail in
Thoreauian contemplation. Families become convenient for celebrities, a quick and easy way of showing selflessness and devotion and
love when they are selfish and devotionless and love only the view in
the mirror. As a writer you become something of a bomb-sniffing dog,
ferreting out the one-in-a-million real from the 999,999 times out of a
million fake. When an A-list actor says he loves his children, that
means he has just gotten off the Percocets and the Oxys and until his
publicist just told him, didn't know the names of his children, much
less the girlfriends and wives who had them. When a politician says
he is quitting the race to spend more time with his family, it means
that the latest poll has given him no chance of winning. When a sports
superstar gives thanks to his family . . . let's not be ridiculous.

It isn't gullibility or cynicism on the part of the writer, just the facts.
But when Albert Pujols invokes his family, there is a softness of awe
in his voice and an ethereal look on his face that frays the common
conception.

When Pujols was eighteen, old enough perhaps to know that he
wanted to be a major-league player but not old enough to really know
much of anything else, he started dating a woman named Deidre. He

liked Deidre. He liked her a lot. He was falling for her, but before it went too far Deidre had to tell him:

She had been in a relationship and had recently given birth to a daughter named Isabella, who had Down syndrome. Deidre could envision Albert's response—running away as fast and as far as he could, no matter how slow his time to first base. Way too much responsibility for a teenager. Way too much responsibility for maybe anyone. It was an understandable reaction, or at least the reaction that Deidre expected.

Instead, Albert married Deidre, knowing that in his vow to her he was making the same vow to Isabella. He embraced the two and has continued to do so, not from obligation or guilt or any other self-disguised trapping but out of the quality that is the most special about Albert Pujols: his heart.

Whispers over his performance will continue. They will become ageless. No matter how many times he says no and itemizes the number of tests, there will always be those who say yes, who will argue, just like they argued he wasn't the greatest when I knew he was, that he cannot be believed. But they are wrong.

The truest measure of a man is not how he performs in the isolated chamber of work but the challenges he is willing to face outside the cocoon. It is there where the intangibles of integrity and honesty reside. I too have a child, now twenty-six, born with significant handicaps. I know the profound beauty of him, just as I know the profound helplessness you as a parent feel. I know the incredible strength of him, just as I know that he is irrevocably and unfairly scarred. I know the joy of him, but I also know the endless challenges of him. I know the pride I feel for him, and I know the tears I cry for him.

I was twenty-six when I faced the reality of my son. So I think often about the willingness of Albert Pujols to inherit what he did when he was eighteen. It's all I really need to know about him. Which is why I believe in everything he has done, everything he has said, and I always will.

In the end the game leaves you, sometimes sooner than a ballplayer anticipates, sometimes later. The home runs and the slugging percentages and the batting averages are heaped to the statistical Everest. Inevitably, somebody does come along who is even better. What remains is the ineffability of character.

The Great Pujols.

Which, ironically as it turns out, has not a thing to do with baseball.

Steve Dembowski
JIM BOUTON

This is the summer that my favorite teammate, Steve Dembowski, now fifty-one years old, would have been inducted into baseball's Hall of Fame. The five-foot-four infielder with the intelligent eyes and the shy smile would have modestly waved to the crowd on his way to the microphone, while his adoring fans chanted just a few of his many nicknames: Dembo, Bull's-Eye, and, of course, Hit Man.

Speaking in his Jersey Guy accent and standing on his toes for comic effect, Dembowski would have begun his remarks by joking about a podium "still calibrated for last year's inductee, Jim Rice." Then he would have had them roaring with delight as he exchanged his New York Mets cap for a batting helmet, an obvious reference to the record that became Dembowski's trademark: Most Times Hit by a Pitch— 595 over a sixteen-year major-league career. (To put that in perspective, Hughie Jennings [1891–1918] was beaned a record 287 times.)

Sensitive to the focus on that one aspect of his game, Dembowski would have gently reminded the fans that he was often among the major-league leaders in runs scored and stolen bases. The only thing he was slow at, as he always used to say, "was getting out of the way."

Yes, Steve Dembowski would have said all of those things and more at his induction ceremony this July (in his first year of eligibility) in Cooperstown—if only they had given the guy a chance.

The Hit Man's distinctive calling came to him in a vision at the end of his senior year, at Rutherford (New Jersey) High School, in 1974. After the last game of the season Dembowski looked in the mirror and saw seventeen black-and-blue marks with lovely shades of purple and mottled yellows, one for each time he had been hit by a pitch. Where most people would have seen bruises, however, Dembowski saw tickets—to the big leagues.

But first he had to make the team as a walk-on at Fairleigh Dickinson University in nearby Teaneck. When he was sent to play left field during fall tryouts, all you could see from the dugout was Dembowski's cap—the top part of it. FDU baseball coach Johnny Orsino, former Baltimore Orioles catcher, described it to a reporter thusly: "Hey, there's nobody out in left field . . . what's going on . . . there's no left fielder . . . just a . . . a . . . damn. There's nothing out there except a baseball cap."

Then the batter swung, and the cap started running backward and disappeared. "I think it just ran through the fence," said Orsino. "Somebody please go find it."

A minute later the cap was jogging back toward the dugout atop Steve Dembowski, who had a smile on his face and the ball in his glove.

Sadly, the cap and Dembowski were both cut from the team. But being cut means different things to different people. To Dembowski it meant returning the following day and taking infield practice wearing jeans and a T-shirt and refusing to leave the field.

"Okay," said Orsino. "Go get a uniform and get back out here."

It may have been the best decision the coach ever made.

Dembowski prepared for the spring season by working out all winter long. This was back in the day when an off-season workout for a ballplayer meant limiting oneself to two beers after a pickup basketball game. Dembowski's workouts, by contrast, would have exhausted Rocky Balboa. Bench presses, leg presses, and curls at a gymnasium. Running for miles every night through the streets of Rutherford, up and down hills, in all kinds of weather. Dembo, of course, remembers it fondly. "I can still see the Christmas lights," he says. "And I remember the smell of smoke from the wood-burning fireplaces. When I reached the Citgo station I would step it up, 'cause I knew I was getting close to home."

By next spring Dembowski was ready to play. Batting seventh in the season opener against George Washington University, across from the White House, he got three singles and a double, stole two bases, and scored three runs. That established him as FDU's leadoff batter for the remainder of his college career. It also earned him the acceptance of his teammates. "During my last at bat in the twelfth inning," he recalled, "one of the players hollered, 'C'mon, Dembo, get on base. Start us off.' You never forget that."

Over the next four years there were many unforgettable Dembo moments, most of which happened to be memorialized by one form of media or another. In a perfect storm of fate and verbiage, it turned out that the FDU sports information director was one Jay Horowitz, a whirling dervish of press releases and salesmanship, who would later become VP of public relations for the New York Mets.

Horowitz had the ability to conjure a story from whole cloth—as long as it had a number on the back. I speak from experience as a former New York City sportscaster (WABC-TV and WCBS-TV) who covered every one of Horowitz's stories. How could I not? Name a season and Horowitz had an angle.

There was Father John Pierce, the Franciscan monk FDU hockey player. And Mal Dixon, the forty-three-year-old FDU field-goal kicker.

And Franklin Jacobs, the five-foot-six FDU track star who jumped two feet above his own height to win the Milrose Games and enter the *Guinness Book of World Records*. What about fencing, you ask? That would be Tom Depoto, the one-armed FDU swordsman whom Horowitz hyped in a press release as having "defeated Rutgers single-handedly."

But for sheer volume of newsprint (and film at 11:00), no one outdid Steve Dembowski. Following his high school vision, the bruise artist continued to work in the difficult medium of getting hit by pitched balls. Why not? Nobody else was doing it. He had the market all to himself!

How good was Dembowski in his area of expertise? He was hit four times in one game and three times in three different games. He was hit in nine consecutive games. He was hit seven times in a doubleheader! And these were not brushback pitches that happened to catch a baggy uniform à la Ron Hunt of the Mets. "Not me," the Hit Man told a reporter. "I don't want to look sloppy."

What Dembowski did required skill as well as guts. A master of the glancing blow, he was not easy to "drill," as the practice is known today. In fact, he rarely needed more than a cursory exam from the trainer and a pat on the ass from the skipper before dusting himself off and trotting down to first base. A slight limp was often followed by a steal of second—a good place from which to steal third.

"I usually try to take the pitch in a safe place," Dembowski said, "like the rear end. Or my left arm, which I don't use. Once in a while I'll get hit in the ribs, but my sister checks it out. She's a nurse."

This was all (chin) music to Horowitz's ears. Come see the Human Target, he proclaimed, like a carny barker under a tent next to the Bearded Lady and the Cardiff Giant. And, ladies and gentlemen, the Human Target can actually play baseball! When he isn't getting hit, he's *getting* hits! And walks! And stolen bases! And he does it all on cue!

Dembowski's specialty within a specialty was getting hit when the cameras were rolling. The bigger the network, the more the Hit Man delivered. At one time or another, he took one in the ribs, elbow, shoulder, or thigh, for Dick Schaap ("NBC Sportsman of the Week"), Bryant Gumbel (*The Today Show*), Warner Wolf (*Game of the Week* pregame show), and a host of local guys at WCBS-TV, WNBC-TV, WABC-TV, plus New Jersey Channel 50.

According to Horowitz, one time there were eleven different camera crews *at the same game.* With all that pressure, the NBC producer Bill Peters expressed concern for Dembowski's safety.

"Tell him to be careful, Jay," said Peters. "If he doesn't get hit today we'll catch him another time."

"Don't worry," said Horowitz, "he'll do good for you."

Providing a little something for everyone, Dembowski did good enough to get a walk, a single, a double, a home run, and hit by a pitch.

At four other games where cameras showed up he was hit eight times, got on base in seventeen of twenty-one at bats, and went ten for fifteen officially. One night I ended my sports segment by thanking Dembowski for coming through for our camera.

"Incredible, unbelievable, unreal," FDU coach Harvey Woods was quoted as saying. "Steve is our table setter. He gets our rallies started. Every time I look up he's on first base. He plays the game with an intensity you can't really comprehend until you sit on the bench next to him."

When Dembowski was hit for the tenth time in his senior year, they stopped the game and presented the ball to his parents. Fortunately it wasn't bloody. Not that his parents didn't have a sense of humor. On a rare stretch when the Hit Man went hitless for three games, his mother (who is four foot ten) came to the ballpark with a sign reading, STEVE MUST GO! "When the One Great Scorer comes to mark against your name," she once said to him, "He writes not whether you won or lost— but how many times you got hit and where."

In his senior year Dembowski compiled an amazing set of statistics: a .375 batting average, with thirty-nine walks, forty-one runs scored, twenty-seven stolen bases in twenty-eight tries (second-best in the nation), twenty-one RBIs, and four home runs. What's more, he was hit an additional thirty-six times, giving him a college career total of 112. With all that hitting and getting hit, the most incredible statistic of all was the Hit Man's on-base percentage: .729.

With stats like that, you probably think Dembowski was drafted by a major-league team in one of the early rounds. But you would be wrong. He wasn't drafted in *any* round.

This was 1978, many years before baseball understood its own statistics (Michael Lewis's *Moneyball*, which proved the importance of the on-base percentage, wasn't published until 2003) and many years *after* baseball stopped understanding the players themselves.

Scouts don't get to know players personally anymore. In 1957, when I played high school ball, a scout would walk you home after a game, meet your parents, become your friend. Now players are just names on a computer printout.

"The scouts didn't really notice him," Woods was quoted as saying. That's because they were looking too high. Scouts are always seeking out big guys, six foot two or better, who can hit with power or throw ninety-five miles per hour. They have stopwatches and radar guns and camcorders that can measure everything—except the size of a man's heart.

Despite all the attention generated by Horowitz—which included letters to Ted Turner of the Braves and Bill Veeck of the White Sox, the two owners most likely to appreciate Dembowski's unique skills— the Hit Man never got a real shot. The closest he came was a two-month stint in a short season Class A League with the Newark (NY) Co-Pilots. Picking up where he left off in college, Dembowski was hit fourteen more times and led the league in on-base percentage. Not enough for the scouts, whose reports most likely included the fact that the Hit Man slept in the luggage rack on the bus rides. Take a hike, son.

My most enduring memory of Steve Dembowski goes back to an early Sunday morning at a ball field in Moonachie, New Jersey, in 1992. I was a fifty-four-year-old pitcher for the Moonachie Braves of the Met League—a very good, no-age-limit amateur hardball league in northern New Jersey—and Steve was the team's player/manager. It had rained the night before, and Dembo was there at 9:00 A.M. sweeping water off the field for a 2:00 P.M. game. I picked up a rake and asked where the other players were.

"Are you kidding?" he said. "It's tough enough to get them to show for the games." He shook his head sadly. "It's not like it used to be."

He was right about that.

It used to be that a guy who loved the game like Steve Dembowski (enough to risk life and limb) would be given a few years in the minors to develop. He would have been in that category of the little, or little-known, players who worked their way up from Class D and made it all the way to the Hall of Fame. Guys like Yogi Berra, Phil Niekro, and Pete Rose, to name a few.

A group that Steve Dembowski, now a highly respected New Jersey detective, would almost certainly have joined this summer.

Kirby Puckett
CRAIG FINN

1984

Like many music enthusiasts of my generation, I look back on 1984 as a banner year. This was the year Prince and Madonna ruled the pop charts and were inescapable in my god-awful junior high school, where I was harassed, depressed, and languishing in the seventh grade. It was also a fantastic year for American underground music, providing me the tiny light by which I marched through these gray days. I had recently discovered two bands in my hometown of Minneapolis, the Replacements and Hüsker Dü, and had become an obsessive fan and record buyer. Both of these bands released landmark records in 1984: the Replacements' beautiful *Let It Be* and Hüsker Dü's sprawling masterpiece *Zen Arcade*. I went to my first all-ages hardcore show that year and tried smoking pot for the first time. Elsewhere— San Pedro, California, and Athens, Georgia, to be exact—the Minutemen had put out *Double Nickels on the Dime* and R.E.M. *Reckoning*. These were exciting new releases to chase. It was a wonderful time to be young and in love with music. It would be some time before I fell in love with life itself (and was able to put my hands on stuff with enough potency to actually get me high), but that's a bit much to ask for a boy still wrestling with puberty.

It was also in 1984 that I first saw Kirby Puckett play baseball. I was sitting in the television room at my friend Matt Johnson's house. He lived down the street from me and knew more about baseball than I did. I was only a casual fan, as the Twins had done little to distinguish themselves in the seven years since my parents had moved to Minnesota from Massachusetts, aside from trading Rod Carew, building a domed stadium, and perpetually hanging around last place. There was no comparison to the local enthusiasm generated by the Vikings or even the feisty North Stars, who reached the Stanley Cup finals in 1981. Minneapolis seemed a pretty poor baseball town, and this was no more evident than when I went back to Massachusetts to visit family—Red Sox scores part of a dialogue that grown men traded back and forth with ease at street corners and restaurants. It was, and I believe still is, a game that makes the most sense on the East Coast. And compared to Fenway Park, the Metrodome was a lousy place to see a game. Thus, at the time, I was probably more a fan of the Red Sox than the Twins.

Also, with my new obsession with punk rock, I wasn't sure how much I really cared about sports anyway. It was the jocks who were giving me such a hard time at school. I was small and bookish, pretty much hopeless in gym class and most other athletics. I was a decent tennis player, but that was because my parents had allowed me a ton of lessons and I considered John McEnroe to be punk in his own way, for his treatment of linesmen and because he played guitar. I no longer equated liking sports with being cool, and the part of my brain that used to obsess over scores and statistics was being filled with information from hardcore fanzines, show calendars, and record jackets. I wanted my identity to be music, specifically underground rock and roll, and watching sports on television in a suburban rec room seemed pretty lame compared to the urban excitement of taking the bus to a show.

(It's interesting to me that now almost every band I meet has at least one huge sports fan in its lineup. In the mid-'80s it seemed like you had to choose one side or the other. At some point that all changed. I think Pavement might have had something to do with it. When they appeared in the early '90s, I felt like I could finally admit that I liked playing tennis more than I liked most indie rock bands. Way more. Pavement were educated young gentlemen having a good time, but you felt like they probably had teams they pulled for. I'd never gotten that feeling about Dinosaur Jr., Black Flag, or the Replacements. Imagine my surprise, then, at spying my teenage hero, Paul Westerberg, at the Twins spring training in 2007. Perhaps rock and roll sports fans have always been there and were just stuck in the closet until *Slanted and Enchanted*.)

At Matt's house that May evening, he informed me that the Twins, as a replacement for disappointing center fielder Jim Eisenreich (later diagnosed with Tourette syndrome), had recently called up a new young player with a great name: Kirby Puckett.

"You gotta see this guy," Matt said. "He's kind of funny looking."

Indeed, you almost had to laugh at the sight of him. He was short, and his butt stuck out like a bubble when he was at the plate. He looked a bit like a fire hydrant and a bit like a teddy bear—cute to match his name. He slapped a single on the first at bat I witnessed and was beaming ear to ear when he reached first base. And oh, that smile. It was like a million watts of bright lights. It was a smile that told you he felt pure joy to be standing on first base, to be playing baseball in the big leagues, to be wearing a Twins uniform. He started jawing with the opposing team's first baseman as if they were old friends. The first baseman looked amused. He couldn't help it. There was something about this guy that was special.

I started watching more Twins games that year. After dinner with my family I would drift into our television room and catch a few innings. They were on almost every night on Channel 9, half innings sandwiched between low-budget advertisements for Plywood Minnesota and Twin Cities Federal Bank. It seemed as if Kirby's arrival had supercharged the team, but in reality it had slowly become well stocked with some great players. As instantly likable as Puckett and already a fan favorite, Kent Hrbek was a local Minneapolis kid who played first base, hit with power, and more often than not wore a devilish grin. Outfielder and sometime DH Tom Brunansky and infielder Gary Gaetti were also great players coming into their own.

In the end, the 1984 Twins finished 81–81, a respectable record for a team that lost more than a hundred games in 1982. They were learning how to win. They had a bright future, with young players and more fan enthusiasm than there had been in years. The Red Sox had lost a fan. I was in love with the Minnesota Twins and the way they played baseball.

1987

I am not sure anyone remembers 1987 more fondly than I do. By then most of my friends had their driver's licenses, so our sense of freedom was widened dramatically. I had switched to a private school for ninth grade and was light-years happier than I had been in my old school. I was succeeding academically and socially. It might not even be a stretch to say that I was popular. I was certainly comfortable in my own skin, having shaken off the awkward depression that haunts the years around puberty.

That summer was glorious. My friend Eddy's car took us anywhere we needed to go. After dinner with our families we would go to Uptown Minneapolis, smoke cigarettes, and listen to street musicians. We started to come across real pot. We went to some killer shows: the Meatmen, the Exploited, Naked Raygun, and our favorite, the Descendents. In July we saw them play First Avenue on their final tour. The show was recorded and released as *Liveage,* one of rock's best live records.

In August my parents surprised me with an impromptu vacation to Cape Cod to celebrate my sixteenth birthday. I came back, took my driver's test, and passed on the first try. Somehow I ended up with a red Mazda RX-7 as my first car. Two seats, five speeds. It was awesome. The day before I started eleventh grade, I drove to see Hüsker Dü at First Avenue. When school started up again I started spending a large amount of my time with a pretty girl who liked the Replacements as much as I did. Oh, and did I mention the Twins were heading toward the pennant? Life was pretty much perfect.

Since the 1984 campaign, the Twins, while long on personality, had yet to fulfill their potential. In 1987, that changed. It was the year the Twins introduced their modern uniforms, and that Phil Niekro was comedically ejected from a game (and suspended ten more) for his use of an emery board. Kirby was the team's sole representative in the All-Star Game and had an American League–leading 207 hits.

Some of those were pretty big ones, too. He had transformed himself from a slap-singles hitter into a power hitter, in the process becoming nothing short of a Twin Cities phenomenon, loved by the whole city. There was magic when he came up to bat in the Dome, with Twins announcer Bob Casey drawing his name out for the rabid fans: "Kiiiiiiiirrrrrrbbbbbby Puckett!" I remember coming out after a rousing win one evening in August to a whole gaggle of kids, roughly six or seven years old, celebrating a birthday party. Each of them wore a T-shirt with Puckett's number 34. Some of them had "Kirby" painted across their cheeks. The chaperone, a young mom, yelled a rhetorical "How about Kirby's home run?!" The kids cheered wildly, as if he'd hit it for them alone, a birthday tribute.

The playoffs came, and it was like nothing else was happening. Not school, not life, not love. Just our Twins. We made quick work of the Detroit Tigers and then faced the St. Louis Cardinals. It was a fantastic series, going to the seventh game. Luckily for the Twins, they had home-field advantage. About fifteen of my friends got together and watched Game Seven in a friend's family room. I was in tears at the victory. It wasn't just that our local team had won; these were *my guys*. I couldn't get over the fact that we were on the cover of *Sports Illustrated* three weeks in a row. When you live in Minnesota, being the center of attention is a sweet but fleeting feeling.

Next came the parade. My school day wasn't cancelled, as many were, but attendance was hardly enforced. We headed downtown to see the players, decked out in ankle-length fur coats in the chilly Minnesota fall, waving at the fans through the confetti, all of us screaming our lungs out. I remember Kirby the most. Again, it was that smile. It radiated and sent straight into my soul a feeling of joy and accomplishment and everything pure and true about that autumn.

1991

I went to Boston College in the fall of 1989. The student body was sports-obsessed, not only with our beloved BC Eagles but with pro sports as well. That said, most kids came from New York, New Jersey, and Massachusetts, and considered Minnesota the end of the world, if they considered it at all. It was hard to keep up with the Twins, and I was also wrapped up in other pursuits: beer, girls, rock and roll, and academics, I guess. I slept through most of the 1991 season and only perked up with the start of the AL Championship.

I got to reacquaint myself with the team while watching it roll over the Toronto Blue Jays. They certainly weren't a collection of marquee names—Hrbek and Puckett still the backbone—but they matched up well with the NL champion Atlanta Braves. I have read many times that this was the best World Series ever played. Being away from Minneapolis, I didn't feel quite the same emotional charge as I did during the 1987 World Series. I mostly watched the games alone in my bedroom, hanging on to little superstitions that got them through tough innings. As would any student at a Jesuit university, I prayed for my team.

I am pretty sure God listened. He certainly helped Hrbek make an unlikely play on Ron Gant at first base and get the controversial call. And divine intervention was certainly at work in Puckett's Game Six heroics. His eleventh-inning home run, which forced a Game Seven, was a career-defining moment. Every Twins fan remembers Kirby circling the bases, pumping his fist. And again, that smile.

My mother and father were at that game and were reportedly high-fiving strangers in downtown Minneapolis afterward. I was in Boston, throwing up. Too much excitement and bad keg beer. I spent the whole next day in bed, and most of Game Seven in nervous exhaustion. Two barely interested friends stopped by and watched most of the game with me, but when we ran out of beer, the scoreless tie became too much for them to take. I was alone when Gene Larkin singled home the winning run. I was suddenly heartbroken that I wasn't in Minneapolis to celebrate.

Watching the postgame celebration, the hugs and locker room champagne, I kept my eyes on Kirby. His joy was shining brightly and dangerously contagious. Just as in 1987, I wept. I now have a DVD of highlights of these Series, and I watch it more than I should probably admit. It still gives me chills. One thing that's great about being an underdog is the elation that goes with winning. As long as the Yankees keep grossly outspending the majority of the competition, no New York fan will ever get to feel what we felt in 1987 and 1991. And I wait patiently for our next title.

2006

A lot happened in the fifteen years that followed the 1991 Series. I returned to Minneapolis from Boston. I started a band and played about one thousand rock and roll shows. The band broke up, and I moved to New York. I started another band: the Hold Steady. People really reacted to our second record, *Separation Sunday*, and by the fall of 2005 I was a very busy man. In February 2006, after a grueling few months, we did our first tour of Australia, and afterward I decided to visit Minneapolis to unwind. Sitting in my parents' house watching television, I saw the news flash that Kirby had suffered a stroke in Phoenix, where he lived. Doctors performed an emergency surgery, but it failed to help. The next day, March 6, 2006, Kirby Puckett died at age forty-five.

Those fifteen years had taken Kirby to a lot of different places as well. His last major-league season had ended abruptly in 1995 with a fastball to his face. In early 1996, while at spring training, he woke up with no vision in one eye. His playing days were over.

I have read that this sudden departure from baseball led him to a depression that may have contributed to his early passing. His weight certainly skyrocketed after his retirement. Both my mother and I had seen him on separate occasions buying large amounts of junk food from a local supermarket (Kirby lived close to my parents). Still, he was his usual charming self when he was inducted into the Hall of Fame in 2001. After ten All-Star Game appearances, six Gold Gloves, and the highest lifetime batting average (.318) of any right-hander since Joe DiMaggio, he had transformed himself from a Minnesota crowd favorite to one of modern baseball's greatest players. At the ceremony, his teammates spoke admiringly of him and fans cheered wildly.

A year or so later, in 2002, Puckett was charged with criminal sexual conduct and assault for an incident said to have occurred at the Redstone Grill in the suburbs of Minneapolis. His attendance there was troubling enough. This is where Minnesota's pro athletes go to meet female fans. The whole place is in heat. He had allegedly pulled a young woman into the bathroom and grabbed her in an inappropriate manner. He was eventually acquitted, but not before causing serious damage to his image. Reports of his infidelities and shocking public behavior began to surface. His wife divorced him. Kirby moved to Phoenix.

It was tough to take. And when he passed away, despite his Hall of Fame career and the fact that he'd spent it with only one team, it was tough to keep his fall from grace totally separate from his death. In the end, we found that he wasn't just a home-run hitter. He wasn't just a home run–robbing fielder. He wasn't a teddy bear. He was a human with problems of his own.

Since I was home the day he died, I drove downtown to the Metrodome to pay my respects. I wasn't alone. There were people all over town walking toward it. A makeshift shrine had been erected at the gates. There were baseballs, gloves, jerseys, and tons and tons of handmade cards and signs. My favorite depicted a pair of cleats cutting into a second baseman's shin. It was captioned "Kirby, teach Ty Cobb fair play." Fans wandered around reading the homemade cards to one another. I dropped my own on the shrine. It simply said, "Thank You, Kirby."

Dave Kingman
CHRISTOPHER SORRENTINO

Dave Kingman came to the Mets from San Francisco. It strikes me as a little odd that the Giants dumped him, because that team found itself lacking in power, for a change. Years of Willie Mays and Willie McCovey and Bobby Bonds were about to become years of Willie Montanez and Bobby Murcer and Larry Herndon. But Kingman seemed never to have developed quite in the way the Giants hoped. He couldn't field. He couldn't really throw (despite having started out as a pitcher). He couldn't even hit, unless someone made the mistake of throwing him a fastball that he could pull over the left-field fence. Pitchers did this frequently enough to make a Kingman at bat a strangely pregnant interval. Things got quiet. It could go one way or another. He might strike out on some outside pitch that even Clemente couldn't have gotten to, or he might rattle the upper deck with a ball hit so hard that you could almost understand why for so many the appeal of baseball seems limited to the showdown between the overpowering strikeout pitcher and the brutally strong home-run hitter. Anyway, the Giants must have had something in mind other than a brief distraction, four or five times a game, from their many deficiencies.

The Mets, of course, in acquiring Kingman after the 1974 season for $150,000, could have had little else in mind.

By the mid-'70s, it was clear that Mets fans were living in a fool's paradise. After the World Series win of 1969, the team's steady mediocrity had been leavened by the 1973 pennant it had managed to snatch amid the sustained domination of the National League by the Pittsburgh Pirates in the East and the Cincinnati Reds in the West; by the presence in the starting rotation of Tom Seaver, Jerry Koosman, and Jon Matlack (who would combine for more than 250 victories during the five and a half seasons they were on the team together); and, maybe most crucially, by the long swoon of the New York Yankees, who had sunk into a kind of cultural irrelevance that many of the team's present-day fans might find unthinkable. There were other good things, too: Rusty Staub, acquired from the Expos in a subtly excellent trade; Tug McGraw, who used to stride out to the mound in relief (after having been driven down the right-field foul line, in the now-quaint manner of the time, in a golf cart) accompanied by an Irish jig played buoyantly by Shea Stadium organist Jane Jarvis; a great defensive catcher in Jerry Grote; and an excellent middle infield—all of which enabled the Mets to crawl over the .500 mark every season from 1970 to 1973.

It probably says a lot about my personality that I think there's a kind of nice, low-pressure fun to rooting for a team that mostly stays in contention and wins occasionally. (The teeth-gnashing and flesh-rending and all-or-nothing howls for blood that are the stock in trade of Yankees fans confirm, at least for me, the reasonableness of that sensibility.) But in 1974—the year Seaver suffered from sciatica and won only eleven games, resulting more or less directly in the Mets finishing twenty games under .500—it was obvious even to me that the Mets weren't going to win anything, not even occasionally, if they didn't get some hitting. When the pitching faltered, the team, which finished tenth or lower (in a twelve-team league) in nearly all relevant offensive categories, had no chance.

This was before free agency—arbitrator Peter Seitz's decision invalidating baseball's reserve clause would come after the 1975 season—so it would have been difficult, even with the mandate as clear as it was, for the Mets to obtain hitting, because it must have been equally clear to the rest of the league what the Mets might be able to accomplish with a decent lineup supporting a superb pitching staff. They managed to pick up, for example, Del Unser and John Stearns from the Phillies but had to trade McGraw to get them. From the Cardinals, they got Joe Torre—or "Brooklyn-born Joe Torre," as the papers liked to remind us, as if his hometown provenance would make up for the fact that he was already well past his prime. Mets chair M. Donald Grant made it perfectly plain that he wouldn't be having any of that free-agent tomfoolery, so the Mets were poised at the edge of the wilderness, a wilderness they would enter soon enough: The icy void at the Mets' heart wasn't in their batting order; it was in the front office. Through pride, lack of vision, and epic chintziness, the project of playing National League baseball at the major-league level in New York City would before long be abandoned for several years in a manner as searing and insulting, in its way, as the wholesale abandonment of the city two decades earlier by the Giants and the Dodgers, even as a simultaneous reversal of fortune was taking place in the Bronx. (Whatever else one may wish to say about George Michael Steinbrenner III, he immediately grasped and embraced baseball's future and the imperatives attendant upon owning and successfully operating a major-league franchise.)

But that's another essay. I suppose anyone looking carefully enough could have seen the darkness beyond the tree line. I wasn't looking. I was eleven, and primed for sideshows. Unser was a slick center fielder.

Stearns was supposed to be the next Johnny Bench. Torre had won the MVP just a few years before. And then there was Dave Kingman.

The Kingman Experience went something like this: Imagine a game in, say, June 1975. I'm watching with my father on the black-and-white Philco console TV in our living room in the West Village. The game is imaginary, which doesn't make it any less representative, or more meaningless: By June the Reds have hit their stride; the rest of the season will be all about their march toward 108 wins and the World Series. The Mets, meanwhile, have just lost eight of nine. With one out and the score tied, Staub hits a single, then moves to second on another single by Torre. Both these guys are about as slow as can be. Up comes Kingman.

"Come on, baby," my father says.

Kingman takes two pitches—a ball and a strike. The center-field camera shows that Staub has taken a minuscule lead off second.

"Come on, Dave," my father says.

Kingman lunges at a fastball that tails away from him, missing the plate, almost in the dirt; his right hand comes off the bat so that his follow-through is one-handed. He staggers a little, less from the force of the cut than the awkward position from which it was taken.

"Oh, for Christ's sake, Dave," my father says.

The next pitch comes in low and on the outside corner; Kingman swings and connects. The crowd shrieks with joy. The camera follows the ball as it crashes into the stands down the left-field line, just wide of the foul pole. We see the fans scattered among the empty seats there scramble to converge on the ball. The pitcher, having survived this horrendous mistake, then throws an off-speed pitch, a pitch Kingman can't lay off; he hits a grounder to the shortstop—"For Christ's sake,

Kingman!"—who tosses the ball to third base, ahead of the plodding Staub, initiating an easy 6–5–4 double play.

Next time up, Kingman, who seems distracted, strikes out looking. He's booed by the remaining fans.

Kingman then comes to the plate with the bases empty in the bottom of the ninth—the Mets behind by a score of, say, 7–3. On the mound is a kid up from Triple-A, filling out the roster for a player on the DL and getting some innings in against this anemic lineup. The catcher, irritated with the kid's shaking off his signs, allows him to groove a low fastball on a 1–2 count—really no reason for it; Kingman's performance working with a pitcher's count like that couldn't possibly have been any good—and this is what Kingman, and all of us, have been waiting for: He plants his back foot, fully extends his arms, and launches the ball toward the visitors' bullpen behind left field, where it lands amid the relievers already thinking about the beer in the clubhouse.

This was Kingman's basic style; I didn't include, say, the error he was more likely than the average left fielder to have made, but it was perfectly clear that he was present for one reason only. When Kingman first strode through the home clubhouse door at Shea, the Mets' reigning slugger, John Milner, had just come off a twenty-homer season, down three from his career high in 1973. In spring training that first year, Kingman hit eight, two more than the rest of the team combined.

Power had never been a big part of the Mets' game, so it had undeniable allure. At twelve, I couldn't distinguish between power and hitting, which seemed indistinguishable from winning, so I was easily drawn to the Dave Kingman Show. Kingman also brought an enigmatic personality, a *difficult* personality, which in the context of professional sports usually means that the player in question isn't terribly keen to feed reporters the quotes they require to round out their stories. Predictably, he and the media had an exhaustingly dysfunctional relationship.* Reporters can get on an athlete who has everything going for him, as *Daily News* columnist Dick Young and others would demonstrate two years later with a successful campaign to drive Tom Seaver from New York, and a guy with a game as limited as Kingman's could be needled, justifiably, for a variety of shortcomings. Back then I didn't pay too much attention to what reporters had to say about baseball and baseball players (that has changed, although I'm still patently uninterested in journalists' concepts of the moral schema of the game as transgressed against by players), but I managed to become aware of Kingman's troubles with the press; and since I tended to identify with people who got ganged up on, this endeared him to me all the more. Kingman, moreover, had an arrogant air, as if he knew that when he connected, he was immune to his critics. At six foot six, with a lean and wiry build, unabashedly long(ish) hair, chiseled features, and a severe glare, he looked to me (and I already thought of ballplayers as existing wholly separately from mere mortals) as if he'd walked off a different drawing board than the rest of the league. Irresistibly, he looked and held himself a lot like Clint Eastwood, another magnificent and unknowable loner with simplistic solutions to complicated problems.

Like the Man with No Name, Kingman moved around a lot, playing for seven teams over his career back when that was weird (and once playing for four teams over three months, which still is weird). While some accounts suggest that Kingman had a less than felicitous touch

---

* Kingman's psychodrama with the media culminated, toward the end of his career, in a notorious 1985 incident when he sent a live rat to a reporter, which pretty much had everything to do with the fact that the reporter was a woman, although it's worth pointing out that the cascades of gallant outrage that flowed from this incident seem to have been equally based on the reporter's gender.

with his fellow human beings, others indicate that he was a perfectly nice guy who liked to keep to himself, an unfathomable if congenial presence ("I really don't know a lot about Dave Kingman. . . . I don't think we saw the real Dave Kingman in the clubhouse or on the field," Matlack later recalled).

This is a simplified portrait, drawn almost entirely from memory. Of course, there were times when Kingman walked, or bunted, or stole bases, or made diving catches in the outfield. There were times when he laughed and joked in the dugout, times when he offered up thoughtful and substantive remarks after a game. There was something else to Kingman, though. I have to explain first that my father had an interesting if completely irrational taxonomy he employed to make sense of baseball—or, if you will, to make sense of the illogical pastime of taking sides. Things often fell into one of two genera: "bush" or "class," his sense of which derived, no doubt, from the chivalric code of the Ebbets Field grandstand. For example, Pete Rose was bush—I can still remember my father shaking his head in annoyance whenever Rose tore up the first-base line after receiving a walk. Clemente was class. Ron Santo was bush, but Billy Williams was class. Henry Aaron was class. Billy Martin was bush. The Yankees were, always and forever, bush. (I have a letter from my father, written after the 1998 World Series, in which the Yankees, fielding one of the great teams of all time, destroyed the San Diego Padres; it explains in compelling detail why these Yankees were, essentially, bush.) The designated-hitter rule, and by extension the entire American League, was bush.

It gives me pleasure to recall my father's ingrained prejudices, so I could go on and on about this. But despite the seeming endlessness of the subject, some people and things were just sui generis or ambiguous enough to end up outside these two categories. Though Kingman, a dead-pull hitter, ordinarily would have been dismissed as bush by my father (and by me; to be clear, my father passed on many of his biases), there was an element of hamartia to his dedication to the home run that exempted him. For Dave Kingman seemed almost helpless on the baseball field when he wasn't hitting home runs. When he did hit one, though, he was as authoritative as anyone who ever played the game. The sight of him doing it made it difficult to imagine how other power hitters resisted the temptation to chase, at each opportunity, this awesome authority: the ability to reduce the other players to bystanders, the ball out of play, every eye on the one man who, having trumped all the subtle ambiguities of the game, runs the bases unhurriedly. There was something epicurean about Kingman's pursuit of power (note the sensuality of Kingman's remarks to Dick Young in 1977: "You can feel it. You can feel the bat bend in your hands. It's a great feeling to just stand there and watch the ball instead of running for first base. That's the one thing I always thought of, the one thing I never got tired of, watching the ball go over the fence"). Baseball as a whole has moved much further in that direction over the years, but by comparison, there is something smugly Stakhanovist about the one-dimensional quality of a ballplayer like Mark McGwire.

It's not a bad thing to never get tired of, not on a team that hit and ran as poorly as the Mets, or any of the even lousier clubs Kingman ended up on, and I think Bill James misses the point when he reports, with manifest disdain, that "77% of Kingman's career value is his home runs, the highest percentage of any player in history." I would round that way up, because while Kingman may have been instrumental in the occasional victory for other reasons, I think that within the anecdotal, antisabermetric vault of remembrance in which players are forever paired with one defining trait, it's righteous to emblematize that binary homer-or-strikeout struggle of the power hitter.

There are rumors that the owners forced Kingman into retirement, conspiring not to sign him after the 1986 season—in which he hit thirty-five homers while batting .210—because the idea of his reaching the five hundred–homer milestone (he retired with 442), and thereby gaining entry to the Hall of Fame, galled them. If there's any truth to these stories, it doesn't seem to me that the owners had anything in particular to worry about—the matter of Kingman's inclusion would be put to a vote by his natural enemies, the sportswriters. But it doesn't hurt to note that the Hall of Fame, like most institutions that set themselves up in the juried and bureaucratic business of canon formation, seems to have been established with the long-term goal of appearing to posterity as both obvious and shortsighted. What Kingman did is worth something, even bull's-eyes painted on some bleacher seats somewhere, a number hanging from the rafters. When the dust settles, he won't emerge as a better player, but what he was particularly good at is centrally important to the way baseball is played today—the changes that have overtaken the game were merely inchoate when he was playing. Kingman, with his low on-base percentage, his lousy fielding, his towering strikeout totals, and his crummy attitude, represents the easy decision: no questions of perjury, no dicking around with asterisks, no wondering which shoo-in will be discredited next, no head-scratching over whether some solid citizen like Carlos Delgado should get in. But I sometimes like to imagine Dave Kingman returning: Kingman on steroids, in some dinky new ballpark with a nice short left-field porch, a career DH; Dave Kingman blasting past the restrictions of any and all "milestones" in an era when the easy primacy of the home run is accepted unquestioningly; Dave Kingman steadily building some unassailable monument—eight hundred homers? nine hundred?—to teach us something about the perils of untroubled credulity.

Neifi Pérez
KING KAUFMAN

Meetings of the Neifi Pérez Marching and Chowder Society are not crowded affairs, but the membership is genuine in its feelings for the banished shortstop.

Well, I'm reasonably genuine.

Put it this way. My regard for Neifi Pérez is as legitimate as Neifi's big-league talent, my fondness for him as real and true as his ability to help a major-league club ever was.

Wait, come back. Neifi Pérez, shunned in Chicago, detested in Detroit, cursed in Kansas City, really was a legitimate big leaguer over a checkered twelve-year career that apparently ended in disaster when he was suspended twice for positive drug tests in 2007. And while I've beaten him up as much as any stathead—even naming a statistic that measures futility after him—and I join in making him scorned in San Francisco, I have also come around to genuinely admiring him. Life is complicated.

When I tell people that Neifi Pérez is my favorite player, I don't exactly mean that I love Neifi Pérez the human being or even some idealized, media-created version of him as a human being, one who does good work in the community or happily signs autographs for the kids or jokes around winningly with the morning guys on the radio.

I'm also not joking, though I will admit that my fascination with Neifi began as a goof.

He began his career with the Colorado Rockies, spending a few years in the starting lineup and producing decent offensive numbers for a slick-fielding shortstop—thanks almost entirely to playing half his games at Coors Field, which aided hitters to a preposterous degree. He needed that boost just to get to decent. For a slick-fielding shortstop.

But people paid less attention to park factors then than they do now, and while any baseball fan knew Coors Field was a pinball machine, most tended to take Rockies stats more or less at face value. Then, on July 25, 2001, Pérez was traded as part of a three-team deal to the Kansas City Royals, for whom the trade boiled down to Pérez for Jermaine Dye, a twenty-six-year-old All-Star outfielder who had been a fine slugger for two years and would continue to be one for the rest of the decade. Dye was the World Series Most Valuable Player in 2005 with the Chicago White Sox. Pérez spent a year and a half in Kansas City hitting not like a slick-fielding shortstop but like a pitcher.

That performance, combined with the idiocy of the trade that had brought him to Kansas City, made him a hated man among Royals fans and a favorite whipping boy of the sabermetric crowd that was just beginning to make itself heard. A slick-fielding, fast-running scrapper who rarely took a walk, got caught stealing entirely too often, and had no power, he was exactly the kind of player the old-schoolers loved—he led the league in sacrifice bunts one year!—and the Bill James disciples hated.

A recent convert to sabermetrics—shorthand for the idea, championed by James, that baseball can be analyzed through objective evidence rather than just listening to wisdom passed down from one generation to the next—I joined in, a little. But it wasn't until he went from Kansas City to my home team, the San Francisco Giants, that I really took an interest in Neifi.

It was in early June 2003, his first and only full season with the club, when I noticed he was a sort of secret weapon. The Giants were a good but not great 26–22 on the days when Pérez made it onto the field. But when he stayed in the dugout, they were 13–1. The Giants were in first place, five games ahead of the Los Angeles Dodgers, and Neifi not playing accounted for the entirety of that difference.

So I invented the Neifi Index, a measure of the contribution a player makes to his team by *not* playing. The Giants had a .542 winning percentage when Pérez played, .929 when he did not. So his Neifi Index was .387 (.929 minus .542). I concocted the Neifi Award, given to the bench player in each league with the highest Neifi Index, and unique among baseball awards in that you or I, if we could only find our way onto a major-league team, would be a shoo-in to win it. I got a couple of funny columns a year out of it.

Giants fans weren't quick to hate Neifi the way Royals fans had been. The expectations were different. He'd been picked up on waivers, not in a trade for a young All-Star, though the team had then signed him to a two-year contract. As that season wore on, mild puzzlement over the Giants spending more than $2 million a year on Pérez turned into exasperation at seeing him take the field 120 times.

Why is he playing again? He's an out machine!

He was even worse in 2004, and the Giants finally released him in August. He was thirty-one. It had been three years since that fateful trade from Colorado to Kansas City, and in that time, in exactly 1,400 at bats, he'd hit seven home runs. Dye had hit fifty-nine over the same period in sixteen fewer at bats. Since Pérez had left Colorado, his on-base percentage hadn't come within a cab ride of .300, the Mendoza Line of that stat, the minimum output required even to be considered lousy.

A few days after the Giants let him go, Neifi signed with the Chicago Cubs, who shipped him to their top farm team in Iowa, where he was three orders of magnitude worse than lousy. But he could still play a sweet shortstop, and the Cubs had the always-injured Nomar Garciaparra at the position. They called Neifi up when rosters expanded in September, and in his first few games he went six for six with a double and, stunningly, a walk.

Garciaparra's injuries flared up, and manager Dusty Baker began writing Neifi's name on the lineup card every day. After two weeks in a Cubs uniform, Pérez was hitting .382, with a .414 on-base percentage and a .564 slugging percentage. These are outrageous numbers. His OPS was .977, 400 points above his career norm.

Garciaparra came back for the last two weeks of the season, and Neifi played sparingly. But he'd earned himself a one-year contract and, with Garciaparra missing a big chunk of the season and then moving to third base, the starting shortstop job for most of 2005.

That April, he started in like gangbusters again. This was a whole new Neifi! Three weeks into the season he was hitting .393, with three home runs and an Albert Pujols–like OPS of 1.028. Then it was over. Over the next three weeks he hit .175 and was typically unproductive at the bat for the rest of '05—though thanks to that first month it ended up being easily the best year of his post-Colorado career. His on-base percentage, .298, came tantalizingly close to qualifying as lousy.

For this, the Cubs signed him to a new contract, a two-year deal that didn't exactly thrill Cubs fans, who, over the course of 154 games played by Pérez, had come around to hating him just as Royals and Giants fans had.

He can't hit! Caught stealing! Why. Is. He. Playing?!

He had two-thirds of a poor season in 2006 before being dealt in August to the Detroit Tigers, who were in a pennant race and had an emergency at second base. Neifi was ridiculously bad down the stretch, yet there he was on the Opening Day roster in 2007—to the howls of Detroit's fans.

Will he ever take a walk?

Somewhere in there, I began to feel for Neifi Pérez. It wasn't his fault managers kept writing his name on the lineup card. And those managers weren't a pack of fools either. Baker and Detroit's Jim Leyland have their critics, but they've each won more than 1,000 games and three division titles. Baker has won a pennant, Leyland two pennants and a World Series—the latter with Neifi on the postseason roster. Felipe Alou, Neifi's manager in San Francisco, won a thousand games, too.

But more than that, I came to appreciate something important about guys like Neifi Pérez. To be a guy like that, to be a guy who makes fans in four cities tear their hair out, to be possibly the single worst regular player in the major leagues in multiple seasons, to last for a dozen years in the big leagues, start more than 1,200 games, get caught stealing an astonishing 45 times in 102 attempts, you have to be a hell of a ballplayer.

The worst player in the major leagues is a hell of a ballplayer.

The worst player in the history of the major leagues, whoever he was, was a hell of a ballplayer.

Neifi Pérez was a hell of a ballplayer.

It's only in the context of the major leagues that the guy with the lifetime OPS of .672 is oh-my-gosh-is-he-playing-again awful.

You see this if you ever watch big-league pitchers, who struggle to hit .100, take batting practice. They drill line drives all over the place. They're the guys in your muni softball league who hit balls over the houses across the street from the park and everyone says, "He must have played pro ball."

You see it when marginal major leaguers drop back down to the high minors and dominate. If Neifi Pérez wasn't my favorite player, my favorite player might be Trenidad Hubbard, a light-hitting outfielder who in ten years got into 476 big-league games with the Rockies, Giants, Indians, Dodgers, Braves—still with me?—Orioles, Royals—almost there now—Padres, and Cubs. But his real achievement, for me, was spending at least part of sixteen different seasons at Triple-A, where he was a consistently solid hitter into his forties.

How would you like to be that guy? Everywhere you go for most of your life, you're the best. As a kid, you're the guy who can play ball. In high school, in the minors, you're a star. There's really only one place in the whole world where you aren't much good, and that's where almost everybody who knows you knows you from the major leagues.

That's life as Neifi Pérez.

We fans buy our tickets and sit in the stands and boo lustily when our team's current Neifi grounds into a double play or gets caught stealing or serves up a three-run homer in a tie game. But really, who are we to judge? We're the tone-deaf knocking the choir, illiterates mocking poetry. The player has to stand out there near first base, waiting for a teammate to bring him his glove and cap, listening to the catcalls of people who couldn't carry his jock.

Then again, the pay's nice.

Pérez was hitting .172—but still with Detroit—in early July 2007 when he tested positive a second time for amphetamines. A first positive test carried no public punishment at the time, a second resulted in a twenty-five-game suspension. Just as that sentence was ending, he was banned for another eighty games for a third positive test. The Tigers released him.

Neifi called the testing process unfair, claiming the positives were a result of his using Adderall, which he said he'd been prescribed for attention-deficit/hyperactivity disorder. He also said all three positive tests had been administered before his first suspension, that he hadn't continued using the drug through the numerous dirty tests.

No matter, really. The bitter stuff of appeals and depositions. It's been more than two years now. His career appears to be over.

Most of those who remember Neifi Pérez at all will remember him as the first major leaguer to be hit with an eighty-game punishment for drugs. For me, his legacy will be his lousiness, the infuriating sight of his name on the home team's lineup card day after day, the greatness required to induce so much rage in so many fans of so many teams.

I'll never forget Neifi Pérez. He was the greatest lousy player I've ever seen.

Roger Clemens
WHITNEY PASTOREK

I grew up in a suburb of Houston called Memorial, a woodsy patch of shaded cul-de-sacs interlaced with wide sidewalks running parallel to ditches where crawfish grew. Modest, sometimes moldy ranch houses were set back on deep lots, close enough for comfort, but not always so close that fences were required; I remember pretending to be a pony over one long summer, galloping through the unbroken string of backyards that anchored the circled block of my neighborhood with no concern for whether or not I knew the people who lived there. Bike riding was encouraged. A few blocks south of us, a cold green lake served as the community pool. I could walk to the mall. For the majority of my childhood, this environment could pretty reliably be referred to as idyllic.

I knew that my family was not wealthy, but I had no real sense of the economic privilege that surrounded us until I got older and started to do the math. By then, I understood my parents had moved us to the outer orbits of a very rich community because the schools were good there, and the streets safe, and those two factors made it worth putting up with a pair of daughters who constantly complained about not being able to afford Guess jeans like everybody else at school. It helped that there was nothing ostentatious about the homes surrounding ours; none of the houses were rubbing it in. A one-story ranch is a one-story ranch, for the most part—until it gets torn down, and its single lot gets subdivided into four, and somebody builds a cluster of identical three-story red-brick monstrosities where there used to be trees.

I cannot say with any certainty that Roger Clemens was the first person to build a McMansion in Memorial, but I do know that the house he built was the first one I ever actively cursed. The thing was grotesque. It reached to the very edge of its property line, which was buttressed by a wall made of the same ugly red bricks as the house, the mortar a fake-toothed white. Looming over the wall was a satellite dish bigger than my bedroom. At that time I was engaged in some form of hardcore financial envy virtually every single day: of designer jeans, of cars on sixteenth birthdays, of exotic vacations, of cable TV. Yet I would ride my bike past Clemens's house and not feel envy, not dream of having money or fame. I would mostly just think about how totally ugly that thing was and wonder why anyone would rather have a satellite dish than a backyard.

I don't really have a favorite baseball player. Not sure why that is, or what the definition of *favorite* is supposed to be. I've loved two teams in my life—the Houston Astros (from birth) and the New York Yankees (1995–present)—and I've certainly *liked* many of the players I've had the privilege to watch. Jose Cruz held his bat funny and hit home runs deep into the Astrodome's gaping maw. Bill Doran was grubby and quick; Mike Scott suitably supernatural. I respect Nolan Ryan's status as a Texas icon, and Craig Biggio won my heartfelt admiration by being the consummate city employee for twenty years. Derek Jeter, Jorge Posada, Mariano Rivera, Bernie Williams, and I arrived in Yankee Stadium at approximately the same time, but my loyalties also extended to imperfect veterans at the end of careers that originated elsewhere: Paul O'Neill talked to his bat; Tino Martinez had a sheepish grin; Chuck Knoblauch needed serious psychological help. My affections were rarely based on the physical, and I've considered sleeping with the enemy only once: Barry Zito, back when he was with Oakland and his curveball was still dropping from the heavens like an eagle-eyed dove. I enjoyed the way these men played. I bought their jerseys, went to see them out of town, cheered for them like an overengaged mom at a Little League game. But is any one of them my *favorite*? Nah. I mostly just like baseball.

But if I *had* to pick a favorite—I mean, if you held a jockstrap to my mouth and a gun to the head of a bunny and made me choose—the man who floats to the top is the one who best encompasses my belief that baseball is a sport of connections, of coincidence, of eerie, spiritual, all-consuming synchronicity. I focus more on the rhythms than the individuals, more on the full season than the specific game, more on how things affect me than the statistical bottom line. I'm hopeless when it comes to facts but can tell you in endless detail how a single moment—a 1986 strikeout in the sixteenth inning with the tying run on first; a walk-off home run into a cold 2001 November night—changed my life. With my freakish emotional responses to the game thus controlling my experience, then, there is one player who symbolizes all the pulmonary edema–inducing highs and lows of the past decade of my life, spent in thrall to two different franchises. That man is Roger Clemens. It kills me to admit it, but it is true just the same. And the way I know this is because Roger Clemens is the only baseball player ever to break my heart.

I know nothing of his early career, except that he was very good. Growing up in Houston sans the aforementioned cable TV (and pre-Internet),

I was held captive to whatever the newspaper could bring, and it never occurred to me I might want to read the box scores or recaps for that other league, the funny one where the pitchers didn't bat. So I missed most of Roger's time in Boston, didn't care when he went to the Blue Jays, and recoiled with none of the horror my Yankee brethren felt when Steinbrenner brought the Rocket to town in 1999. (I saved that for when Jason Giambi showed up.) Clemens was nowhere near his best those first two years in the Bronx, but he helped the Yanks to Series wins, thus "becoming" a Yankee, that bizarre, undefinable hoop that anyone who puts on the pinstripes must at some point jump through. Since Nolan Ryan's strikeout record was clearly safe, I applauded Rog's effort to rack up K after K, blowing that speedball by batters, making 'em look like fools. I giggled at his bravado, marveled at his competitive drive, wondered at his girth—that strange, genetically Texan phenomenon where the men work out constantly but somehow just get *wider*. I was there for a couple of his trademark almost milestones. September 10, 2001, sitting in the upper deck, hoping to see him go an unprecedented 20–1 by defeating the Red Sox—that game never began, called on account of rain, so much rain it makes the next morning's perfect blue sky seem that much more ominous now. Memorial Day 2003, sitting up the third-base line on another inclement afternoon, hoping to see him win his three hundredth, again against the Red Sox—that game eventually got played, but after a long rain postponement and much ado about the nothing of his ridiculously cocky "300" glove, Roger literally froze up during a third delay (the dreaded National Moment of Remembrance) and left in the sixth with a loss.

I should have known after those two letdowns that my relationship with the guy was cursed. And after Clemens closed out '03 with a triumphant two-month nationwide tour of standing ovations, capped by an awkward final exit—slinking away after giving up four runs in four innings to Boston in what will forever be known as the Aaron Fucking Boone Game Seven of the ALCS—he should have known to stay retired.

Luckily, smug hindsight and five bucks will get me a sandwich.

In 2004, the Yankees let Andy Pettitte get away, and he came home to my Astros, trailing in his wake none other than one enthusiastically unretired Rocket, as though the old Warner Bros. cartoon was reversed and giant bulldog Spike was the one trying to get the scrawny mutt to go chase cats. Clemens was home, and he was more Texan than ever, jumping into local charities, sending his K-named children to my old public high school, practically acting as tour guide during that season's Houston-based All-Star festivities before embarrassing the hell out of himself by giving up six runs in like five minutes to start the actual game. Who cared? He won the Cy Young that year, the first Astro since Mike Scott to pull that off.

Looking back, this *also* would have been a fine moment for Roger to retire, but we begged, and we pleaded, and we threw lots of money at him, and he came back for 2005, and it was completely worth it. Completely worth it for his career-best 1.87 ERA. Completely worth it to watch him glare over his glove for another season, steam coming out of his nostrils just like the longhorn steer that used to light up the awesome old scoreboard in the Dome. Completely worth it, if only for the three innings he pitched in relief during the eighteen-inning playoff marathon we endured against the Braves, trying to get into the NLCS, trying to get, finally, to the Series. In those three innings, Clemens was everything he'd ever claimed to be: tenacious, selfless, a force to be reckoned with. In that moment—for whatever it's worth—he "became" an Astro. We won that eighteen-inning game largely because of the gutsy heroics for which Roger Clemens would prefer to be remembered. When Chris Burke's game-ending home run dropped into the Crawfish Boxes, I tumbled off the coffee table where I'd been crouched for hours and collapsed on the floor, thanking the good Lord above for Number 22. It would be the last time that ever happened. In the first game of the only World Series my hometown team has ever reached, Clemens slunk out of the second inning with a pulled hamstring. We got swept by the White Sox. Naturally, I had tickets to Game Five.

Clemens technically returned in 2006, after the addled brain of Astros owner Drayton McLane ran the numbers and decided, Yes, it *does* make excellent fiscal sense to pay this guy the gross domestic product of Argentina to play just the back half of the season. We *totally* should gut our farm system in order to afford this. Then Rog pulled the exact same stunt in 2007 with the Yankees, because the only man more willing than Drayton McLane to throw good money after bad is George Steinbrenner. Not surprisingly, Clemens disappointed in both arrangements, his pulled hamstring making almost more starts than he did.

For me, this whole saga was a little bit like watching some charismatic asshole wine, dine, and systematically demoralize my two best girlfriends, while making the girls pay for the wine and the food. I so badly wanted it to work out for them, but deep down I knew it never would. Still, I merrily rationalized it all away: Roger got paid millions of dollars to never quite meet expectations as a mercenary of the highest order? Free agency means never having to say you're sorry! He distracted two teams for four straight seasons with the incessant will-he-or-won't-he media circus of the Roger Retirement Rotisserie? A man's got the right to change his mind! He led my beloved Astros to their one and only World Series berth while allegedly under the influence of god knows what? Just slap that joy with an asterisk and move on! Besides, everybody else was doing it!

Which brings us to December 13, 2007, when Clemens was named as a consumer of banned substances by the Mitchell Report, a not-all-that-shocking revelation that inspired countless investigations (journalistic and otherwise) and at least two books I refuse to read on the grounds that they'll make me too sad. His aggressive public stance after the allegations was clear: He did *not* take any banned substances, he resents the implication, and how dare you. But I don't believe him. And that's where the heartbreak comes to rest, finally—not because he injected himself with some shit they put in cows, but because in all my rationalization, the one thing I cannot come to terms with is lack of character, the sort of hubris it takes to deny something so obviously documented by Congress and tell-all memoirs and clubhouse hearsay and photographs in which Clemens's biceps are bigger than Lance Berkman's thighs. I cannot respect the kind of man who lets his trainer, his good friend, and his *wife* take the fall for his actions. His testimony and subsequent media appearances—beady-eyed, self-pitying affairs, all—have only served to reinforce my deep-seated disgust at the entitlement of rich southern white men and, weirdly, to stir up some residual rage about the Bush administration. And seriously, how much stubbornness does it take to watch the American public let Pettitte, Giambi, Jose Canseco, and freakin' *A-Rod* off the hook for the same debatable offense, but refuse to accept that forgiveness for yourself?

It all goes back to our old suburb of Houston, where it's possible he built a monument to his future career before anyone saw it coming: Instead of buying a modest home with a big, shady backyard where kids could gallop around like ponies, he razed the land and erected a McMansion, pushing everything to the edge, blocking out the sun, always wanting more, more, more. He installed a giant satellite dish where there should have been trees, and then he built an enormous red-brick wall with fake-tooth mortar that no one bothers to peek over anymore, because the wall tells us everything we need to know. To look at him now is not to see money or fame, talent or hard work, passion or God-given ability. Now there is nothing to say but, Man, that thing is ugly. And there goes the neighborhood.

Tony Horton

SCOTT RAAB

I started with an outdated home address 3,000 miles away, traced him to a job he left long ago, made a few more calls, and there the trail ended. It wasn't necessarily to write about him that I tried to get in touch, but because I owe Tony Horton something important.

If you're not middle-aged, not from around Cleveland, and you've heard of Horton, it's likely thanks to YouTube, where you can watch a black-and-white clip from the second game of an Indians-Yankees double-dip played back on June 24, 1970. It's preserved because a journeyman Yanks reliever, Steve Hamilton, threw a pitch he called the Folly Floater—an eephus ball he would toss twenty-five feet or so up into the air. In the top of the ninth, with the Indians up 7–2, Hamilton offers two consecutive floaters to Horton.

You can see his body torque as he takes two mighty uppercut hacks. He fouls the first one into the seats behind home plate. He pops up the second one, too, also foul; this time, though, Yankees catcher Thurman Munson has room to make the grab.

The Yankee Stadium crowd roars, and Phil Rizzuto, calling the game, does his "Holy cow!" thing. Horton, meanwhile, crawls on his hands and knees back into the Indians' dugout. He looks for all the world like a kid having fun playing ball, not a guy on some precipice of horror and oblivion.

Truth is, he was a fine ballplayer, with far more stick than glove. "This kid is a natural," Ted Williams said in 1963, after seeing Horton hit at Red Sox camp. "You don't fool with a swing like that." He made it to The Show at nineteen with Boston, got stuck behind George "Boomer" Scott, a far better first baseman, and was dealt to Cleveland for Gary "Ding Dong" Bell in early June 1967. In an era dominated by pitchers, he was the best hitter in a piss-poor Indians lineup. In 1969— the year baseball lowered the mound to aid hitters—he belted twenty-seven home runs. The team finished 62–99.

That off-season, Horton wanted a bigger bump than the front of-fice was willing to give him. His agent was his father. At a time when newspapers essentially owned sportswriters, he was roundly por-trayed as a greedy, young, me-first punk for holding out during the first three weeks of spring training in Tucson. Then he came to terms: the team's.

By the end of May, the Tribe was 16–27, Tony Horton was batting .238, and I was royally pissed off—at the Indians in general, and at Horton in particular. Fucking furious I was.

I know now—thanks to the miracle of baseball-reference.com— that he was hitting a *productive* .238. I know now—thanks to Bill James and a hundred others—that he was something of a jewel: a very good hitter at a very young age. And I know now—thanks to many dollars of therapy and great good fortune—that in 1970 I was a dickweed, an eighteen-year-old no-account shitheel.

All I knew then—all I really wanted to know—was who wanted to go to the game with me and could I borrow the car and a few bucks from my mother. I didn't have dates—I didn't know any girls. I didn't have a job. Didn't have a clue. I had spent most of the best days of my life to that point at Municipal Stadium, a place I always loved, watching some of the least interesting, most inept ball clubs ever assembled, sitting in two-dollar seats among a throng—an exceedingly tiny throng—of humanity so vile it would've gagged Emma Lazarus. I was there not only because I loved baseball and hot dogs; I was there also—and I'm certain that I speak for most of us in Section 34, lower deck, hard by the left-field foul pole and, not incidentally, the visiting team's bullpen—simply because, win or lose, hot or cold, it was a far better place than home to kill a few hours.

Tony Horton made it to the majors at the age of nineteen; I had other gifts. I was loud. Jesus, was I loud. With 5,000 or so fans in a ballpark that held 80,000, I'd holler "HOT DOGS!" when my belly growled, and vendors would race from five or six sections away to serve me. I hadn't learned to drink yet, but I had learned to curse, and sitting near the opponents' bullpen gave me ample opportunity to practice. I never have forgotten my very first one-on-one chat with a big leaguer, a backup catcher for the Angels named Tom Egan.

I'd been riding one of his teammates pretty hard, an old shortstop named Ray Oyler. Strictly a banjo hitter, Oyler was ready for the pasture; he was down in the pen just to help warm up relievers. I don't think he even stole a glance at me as I reminded him several times what a piece-of-shit hitter he had always been, but between innings Egan came up to the low wall at the foul pole, staring at me all the way.

"How old are you, bush?" he asked.

I told him.

"How much money you make?"

I told him.

"I got more money for signing than you'll ever make in your life," he barked. "So shut the fuck up."

I did.

But not for long. I was too far away from first base to ride Tony Horton, so I had to pick my spots. On Camera Day—do teams still dare to
hold an event where fans can get close enough to take pictures?—I threw
pennies at him from the back of a crowd of folks snapping photos.

"Here you go, asshole," I shouted. "Here's the rest of your fucking
money."

If our eyes ever met, I don't remember it.

The evening before the 1970 season's Banner Day—do teams still let
fans hold a pregame parade in the ballyard holding aloft their homemade tributes to their heroes?—I spent an hour or two in the garage
preparing for the event with my friend Ken, my little brother Bob, and
a large sheet of plywood.

First we painted "HORTON STINKS" in big black block letters. (I
recall no debate among us about the wording, probably because
"sucks" was not in common usage yet.) Then we took an old bedsheet
and painted "GO TONY" on it.

It was a simple plan, well executed. Before going downtown to the
stadium, we tied the bedsheet over the plywood and kept it there while
we stood in line outside the park with our fellow Banner Day cele-
brants waiting for the gates to open. Not till we were through the tunnel, past the bleachers, and walking onto the outfield warning track
did we whip off the sheet.

I want to pause here to say this: I have absolutely nothing to say in
my defense. Not a word. Tony Horton could have gone on to forge a
Hall of Fame career; the Indians could've built a baseball dynasty; the
city itself might somehow have become something other than a national
joke—none of it would have made any difference. I know this because
I left Cleveland for good in 1984 yet am still incapable of watching the

Indians—and the Browns and the Cavaliers—play a meaningful game
without reverting to precisely the same awful behavior.

I suspect, now that I dwell in North Jersey among the loutish rabble
of Yankees fans, that I'm not alone in this. Which doesn't make what I
did right. I was the real asshole.

As I remember—I've consulted both Ken and Bob—our work won
wide approval from the Tribe fans already seated. Certainly no Indians
official or proxy interfered with our long circuit; as I remember, we got
plenty of laughs and applause from every section, and a few smiles
from the players in the visiting dugout. I don't remember the response
from the Tribe's. It may be that I was too cowed to look; I'd never been
on a major-league field—haven't since—and my heart was racing. But
this much I know: Tony Horton didn't play that day.

As I remember, Banner Day was Saturday, August 29, 1970. The
day before, after having been yanked from the lineup in the fifth inning
of game one of a twi-night twin bill, Horton had driven back to the
motel where he lived and, sitting in his car in the parking lot, slit his
wrists. On Banner Day he was in the hospital. He lived; his career died.
He never played baseball again.

I hadn't given Banner Day 1970 more than a passing thought for
decades, until a couple of years ago, when Ken sent me a link to Terry
Pluto's estimable book, *The Curse of Rocky Colavito*. There, on page
127, was a short description of our "HORTON STINKS" escapade.

The Tony Horton Pluto portrays was just a kid so bent on being
perfect that he couldn't handle failure, not exactly a plus for a guy in
the big leagues. "He never smiled," a teammate told Pluto, "even after
he hit a home run. . . . I had heard about guys taking batting practice
until their hands bled, but I never saw it until Tony."

Pluto—who grew up in Cleveland and has covered sports for the *Akron Beacon-Journal* and the Cleveland *Plain Dealer* for decades—summed it up by saying, "To me, the most tragic Indian was Tony Horton."

Maybe so—that's what I thought when I read Pluto's book—but the competition is pretty stiff. I pay to sponsor the Larry Doby page on baseball-reference.com, as well as Sam McDowell's and Ray Chapman's. You can read the twisted history of Cleveland Indians baseball in those three names alone: the only major leaguer killed by a bean-ball; the filthy southpaw who guzzled away a potential Hall of Fame career; and the noble sap doomed to eternity in Jackie Robinson's shadow.

I could sponsor Herb Score's page, too, and Steve Olin's, and Ray Fosse's, and a dozen or two other tragedies, but I'm trying to put a little money away for my kid's college tuition. What I'm saying is that being a lifelong Indians fan transcends any of the whining from Wrigley Field or, once upon a time, Red Sox Nation. Pussies. For most of my life, the Indians had neither stars nor hope—only agony. With apologies to Bernard Malamud, to be a Cleveland fan is to suffer, and to suffer is to be a Cleveland fan.

So it seemed to me a reach to deem any single Tribal tale of woe the most tragic. But it wasn't until I began looking for Horton that I learned he had tried to kill himself—his attempted suicide going un-reported until the New York *Daily News* wrote about him in 1997, after the Mets' Pete Harnisch left the team because of depression.

That writer, Bill Madden, visited Tony Horton's Los Angeles home—the ten-year-old address I started my own search with—and was met at the door by Horton's father.

"He won't want to talk to you," he said.

Then Tony Horton appeared.

"I'm not interested," he told Madden just before he closed the door. "You mean a sports story? I'm definitely not interested."

I'm not enough of a drama queen to tell you that Tony Horton and my memories of the 1970 season haunt me, or that I sought to salve my guilt or redeem my sin by finding him. Which isn't to say that I don't regret my assholery—I do indeed—but that as my personal pantheon of cruel and shabby behavior goes, this ain't exactly the star attraction.

And yet.

One of the worst parts of being a devoted fan of any crappy team, in any sport, is the sense that you're truly only rooting for the laundry, that the players in the uniform bearing the name of your town don't care half as much as you do. Nor should they. They may be men playing a boy's game, but they're also men at work at a job defined by its naked difficulty. Their every act is literally numbered, and those numbers—and, in a fan's eyes, the players themselves—are public property. Ultimately, though, they owe us nothing beyond their best effort.

And us? I don't know that fans owe players much of anything. Then again, I'm from Cleveland: I've been suffering all my life. I always figured that since I bought my tickets with my mother's hard-earned money, I was entitled to do pretty much whatever I wanted at the games. And though I realize now how wrong I was, that's merely an intellectual construct that still gets swept away by the flood of feeling that defines my fandom. If you put me, Jose Mesa, and John Elway in a room with a loaded gun, I'm the only one who's walking out alive.

But I do know what I owe Tony Horton, who always gave the Indians his best and paid way too high a price:

I'm sorry, pal.

Jeff Kent

JOHN ALBERT

The story of how I came to respect and even begrudgingly admire Jeff Kent's mustache is in some ways the story of my life. Some might say that my ability to make peace with Kent and his soup strainer saved me. Others would insist that the two of them compromised and ultimately defeated me—that I have sold out and gone soft. I'm sure there is some truth to that. But then again, I'm still alive, and that counts for something.

In order to understand this conflict, some history is in order. The 1970s of my childhood were times known for many things—Vietnam, disco, the Iranian hostage crisis. But primarily they were the golden age of the American mustache. It was a time when a neatly trimmed patch of hair on a man's lip meant something. (It meant something on a woman too, but not the *same* thing.) And to clarify, a real mustache only truly existed unaccompanied by a beard or long hair. There was nothing kindred about a man with a mustache and a hippie. Hippies embraced peace and love, while mustache men embraced apple pie, beating the shit out of hippies, and baseball.

Which brings us to the great American pastime. In the '70s a proper baseball uniform consisted of a jersey, pants, cap, and mustache—and unless you were Oakland A's pitcher Rollie Fingers, who sported an exaggerated twisting handlebar that required its own ragtime sound-track, decidedly nonindividualistic mustaches of the sort found on the actor Burt Reynolds and in countless Marlboro ads.

I was eleven years old the first time I came into contact with said foliage. It was riding the upper lip of my scowling Little League coach. Teams in the Los Angeles suburbs were divided into divisions accord-ing to skill level. My team, the Hawks, resided in the lowest division. It was a stratum reserved primarily for kids with severe birth defects; budding perverts, artists, and drug addicts; and our coach's son Doug, a lumbering dullard with the body of a grown man and the intellect of a house plant.

The coach hated me from the start. He didn't appreciate my long hair, pregame pot-smoking regimen, or the fact that I ran away from the ball if it was hit even remotely in my direction. As punishment, he tried to make me the catcher for his oafish son, our only pitcher. But every time Doug hurled the ball I would immediately dive out of the way, let-ting the ball strike the old umpire in the chest, stomach, and occasion-ally in the face. After an inning, the ump was muttering threats. He eventually stood up, ripped his mask off, and demanded the coach get me the hell out of there. I distinctly remember the coach's mustache trembling with rage as I sat to take off the pads, and the ultimately prophetic words, "You're nothing but a goddamned punk, Albert."

My Little League career ended the following week. I was in right field daydreaming and failed to notice a fly ball hit my way. The ball landed in the grass next to me, jarring me from my fantasies just in time to see the coach, his dolt son, and several of the other musta-chioed fathers screaming angrily. I'd had enough. When the inning ended I sullenly packed up and left. I was done with baseball. I gave away my prized card collection and threw my Dodgers bobble-heads into the trash. From then on it would be subversive rock and roll, drugs, and sex (which at the time meant hiding in a shrub and ogling stolen copies of *Oui* magazine).

But quitting baseball by no means ended my contact with the mustache world. The only subculture with a higher percentage of crumb catchers (other than, of course, leather-clad homosexuals) was law enforcement. Unfortunately, I'd have plenty of exposure to the police following my departure from Little League.

My criminal career had begun a few years earlier with daily shoplifting and acts of senseless vandalism, including hurling rocks at cars, stealing Mercedes-Benz hood ornaments for use as kung-fu throwing stars, and once ringing a doorbell and pelting an elderly wheelchair-bound woman with eggs. (The latter I still view as troubling.) My first formal visit from the fuzz was in the fifth grade and involved some explosives and switchblades purchased across the border in Mexico by a classmate named Chachi. The second was months later and involved a failed scheme to plant marijuana in the kindergarteners' vegetable garden. My friends and I were betrayed by a duplicitous hippie teacher's aide. Two mustachioed cops arrived and yanked us out of class. They took us down to the station and threatened us with juvenile hall, but as their lone witness resembled Pigpen from the Grateful Dead, the case quickly crumbled. It was a pattern that would only worsen with puberty.

By all accounts, Jeff Kent had no such problems with the authorities growing up. A few years younger than me, he lived thirty miles away in Huntington Beach. He came to his mustache by birthright. Whereas my father was a Jewish psychology professor who occasionally wore a false mustache (true story), Kent's was a motorcycle cop. Far from rebelling against his boot-clad father, Kent reportedly idolized the man. He has even publicly stated that some of his fondest childhood memories were "wiping down my dad's motorcycle with an old T-shirt." For context I suggest a viewing of the Pasolini film *Salò*. Bring the kids.

The Huntington Beach of Kent's youth was an exciting place. The high school he attended, Edison High, was ground zero for the convergence of surfing and punk culture. Although the whole thing has long since morphed into something heinous involving wallet chains and middle-aged goons with tattoos, in the late '70s and early '80s cutting your hair and listening to bands like the Buzzcocks was new and revolutionary. Edison was nicknamed Punk Rock High and boasted an assortment of popular bands as well as more than a hundred crop-topped, stage dive–inventing young surf punks.

Kent wasn't having it. He may have lived in Surf City, but he yearned for the cowboy life. While the locals were worshiping at the altar of Sid Vicious, a young Kent idolized none other than John Wayne. (He still boasts about getting the Duke's autograph.) Not able to grow an actual mustache because of his youth and lack of swarthiness, Kent still managed to make his high school baseball team—that is, until senior year, when the urban cowpoke was thrown off for arguing with his coach. With no scholarship offers, Kent chose to attend, of all places, the University of California, Berkeley. (Why he would decide on a school renowned for hippies, nudism, and the Unabomber is one of the great mysteries of our time.) He made it onto the Cal baseball team as a walk-on and began working evenings at a nearby Home Depot. He claims it was there that he first grew his legendary nose neighbor. Reports of him strolling the Castro district in buttless chaps and a Civil War cap during this time have long been considered suspect.

It should be noted that at this juncture, Kent's life and my own could not have been on more divergent paths. After leaving high school, I took some classes at city college, worked at a liquor store, and developed a drug habit. Kent, on the other hand, was drafted by the Toronto Blue Jays. I continued to be arrested, began entering rehabs, and contracted several strains of hepatitis. He was traded to the New York Mets. You get the picture. . . .

But as poorly as my life was going, all was not perfect in Kent's world either. When he arrived in New York, his Met teammates pulled a traditional prank on the newcomer, breaking into his locker and swapping his street clothes for some decidedly less redneck attire. Unwilling to appear fashion-forward for even a night, genetically humorless Kent erupted in anger. As a result, the entire team refused to speak to him for the rest of the year. Far from being an aberration, this sort of conflict was the norm throughout his career. Kent has repeatedly stated that he wasn't in baseball to make friends, and he wasn't kidding. The guy makes a shit like Roger Clemens resemble Groucho Marx.

My long-standing moratorium on baseball finally ended in 1988, the year the Dodgers won the World Series. Kirk Gibson's gimpy walk-off home run and Orel Hershiser's masterful pitching were just too much to resist. Casual interest developed into full-blown obsession during the late '90s, when I began to play ball again in a city hardball league. It was at this time that I first became aware of Jeff Kent. He had been traded from Cleveland to the San Francisco Giants, and quickly achieved the status of my least favorite player on my least favorite team.

Of course, the Giants are the Dodgers' historical rival, but there are additional reasons I've always disliked them—the main one being Barry Bonds. It's not the fact that Bonds cheated. We now know that a majority of players in his era used performance-enhancing drugs. It's the hypocrisy. The people of San Francisco love to rail against Los Angeles as an amoral wasteland of unbridled ambition and narcissism. Having lived in the Southland my entire life, I won't argue that. But the sanctimonious Giants fans knew full well that Bonds was cheating and supported him simply because it served their self-interests. The same can be said of Kent and all those good liberals cheering for a self-styled redneck simply because he was wielding a hot bat.

When Kent was traded to the Dodgers I vowed that I would continue to loathe him regardless. As far as I was concerned, his only worthwhile accomplishment in baseball had been physically attacking Bonds in the Giants' dugout. But with the opportunity to watch him over the course of many months, I slowly began to change my opinion of Kent and gradually started to appreciate the mustachioed one—not despite his faults but *because* of them.

I liked that he said whatever he wanted. During an interview he remarked that beloved Dodgers announcer Vin Scully "talked too much," and when most were hiding behind the players' union on the steroid issue, he openly rallied for stronger tests. He may have been joyless and combative, but he was forthright in an arena of rampant insincerity. When writers mocked his mustache, Kent simply replied, "That's the best you've got?" As rebellion and individuality are increasingly co-opted to the point of irrelevance, there is something inspiring about an old-school asshole.

I was at Dodger Stadium that October night for the final game of Kent's long career. Sensing the importance of the moment as he approached the plate for the very last time, I stood up and began to applaud. Then suddenly I was fighting back tears. I watched with no small degree of emotion as he failed to swing at strike three and was called out. He then turned and simply walked back into the dugout. There was no fanfare, no handshakes or high fives from his teammates. A Hall of Fame–worthy career just . . . ended.

Later, as I left the stadium and headed through the parking lot, I caught my reflection in a windshield and had to smile. There, resting comfortably below my nose, was a mustache.

Jackie Robinson
ROGER KAHN

The volume sits on my mantle, worn by almost fifty years of reading and revisiting, always with affection. Echoing the famous, desperate cry of Brooklyn Dodger fans, the book is called *Wait Till Next Year*. The author has graced the title page with an inscription, dated December 6, 1961.

To Roger with respect and admiration. It has been good knowing you and working with you over the years.

The words are signed—with a large capital J—*Jackie Robinson*.

I pick up the battered old volume, bound in black and a little frayed, and emotions surge.

Pride, of course, that Jack and I were friends.

Enthusiasm. How wonderful it was to watch him play baseball.

Anger. Bigots forever were assaulting him with hate.

Sorrow. White-haired before his time, he died at the age of fifty-three.

Then, finally, an almost spiritual happiness. America at last is realizing that there, on the now paved-over soil of Ebbets Field, stood a hero, strong and indomitable in combat, caring and compassionate after the games were done.

On April 15, 2009, which the lords of baseball proclaimed Jackie Robinson Day, every major-league player was directed to wear Robinson's number, 42. This was a perfect instance of glorious excess. Robinson was first and foremost an individualist, playing with a style wholly his own. Dabbing his number on hundreds of jerseys from San Diego to Boston runs counter to that reality. But it is mean-spirited to decry efforts within baseball to celebrate the man and his legacy.

It wasn't always that way, even in Brooklyn. Jack had a dynamic, sometimes confrontational manner, as opposed to the diffident style of such other early black major leaguers as the great Dodger catcher Roy Campanella. Walter O'Malley, The Big Oom, who ran the Brooklyn club, preferred his hired hands to be servile.

Robinson played in Brooklyn for ten years, batting an aggregate .311, stealing 197 bases. I can't precisely say how many pitchers he rattled with his adventurous base running, but a sound guess is every pitcher in the league. Going clear back to 1900, before Robinson reached Flatbush, the Dodgers had won only four pennants. With him aboard, the Brooklyn team won six. Jack could run and hit and steal and intimidate, and he emerged as the remarkable leader of the remarkable team that I called, in my 1972 book, *The Boys of Summer*. (Patent applied for; royalties cheerfully accepted.)

Numbers cannot capture passion, and passion was at the core of the way Robinson played—and, in point of fact, lived. If I had to pick a single day that displayed his various gifts (and I believe I do), that would be September 30, 1951, the last afternoon of the regular season, when the Dodgers and the Philadelphia Phils played what could very well be the most exciting ball game in the annals.

This was a strong Philadelphia team, which had won the pennant the year before. That autumn the Dodgers were scrambling, having lost a thirteen-and-a-half-game lead to the New York Giants and, as

the Philadelphia game progressed, actually falling a half game behind
the Giants, who defeated the Boston Braves. In the words of Roscoe
McGowen of the *New York Times*, Robinson had been "an early bust."
With Pee Wee Reese at third and Duke Snider at first in the opening
inning, he bounced into a double play. Next time up he looked at a
called third strike. In between, he failed to come up with Richie Ash-
burn's hard grounder, which went for a two-run single. ("Bad scoring,"
Robinson said later. "I should have been charged with an error.")

The Phillies moved ahead, 6–1, and were still leading at 3:35 P.M.
when the Giants' victory was posted on the scoreboard. From his
perch at second base, Robinson looked over his shoulder. Quite simply, it was do or die. If the Dodgers were beaten, they would suffer
what McGowen called "the most disastrous flag loss in National
League history."

In the top of the eighth the Dodgers at last drew even, 8–8. Now
runs, so plentiful early on, became a rare commodity. In the last half
of the twelfth inning, the game still was tied, but the Phillies loaded
the bases with two out. Then Eddie Waitkus lashed a line drive just to
the right of second base. In his New York *Herald Tribune* column, Red
Smith memorably described what happened next.

"The ball is a blur passing second base, difficult to follow in the half
light, impossible to catch. Jackie Robinson catches it. He flings himself
headlong at right angles to the flight of the ball. For an instant his body
is suspended in midair. Then, somehow, the outstretched glove inter-
cepts the ball, inches off the ground." Smith never forgot Robinson
"stretched at full length in the insubstantial twilight, the unconquerable doing the impossible."

Jack wrote the final act two innings later. Facing Robin Roberts, the
Phillies' ace and arguably the best pitcher in baseball, he drove a long
home run into the upper deck in left field. Final score: Dodgers 9,

Phillies 8. "Two more dramatic events—the catch and the home run—probably have never been seen in such a ball game," McGowen pronounced in the *Times*. "Just goes to show ya," Irving Rudd, a peppery Dodger publicity man, said when at length the cheering stopped. "If a game lasts long enough, Jackie Robinson will win it for you."

A decent respect for history impels me to report that the Dodgers promptly lost the playoff series to the Giants on Bobby Thomson's famous ninth-inning home run. An enduring image remains: Robinson holding his defensive position, motionless, hands on hips, making sure that Thomson touched every base.

I began covering the Dodgers regularly the following spring, and seeing up close how good these ballplayers were touched me, a one-time sandlotter, with awe. That has never vanished. I still marvel at how hard the major leaguers swing, how quickly they move, how powerfully they throw. But along with awe came a strong feeling of distaste. I had heard about racism in the American South. Now I was living it. The grandstands at every Florida ballpark were segregated. Hotels would not accept people of color. Public restrooms were segregated. There were separate taxicab companies for whites and blacks. Even water fountains in the parks were marked "white" or "colored."

In the midst of this apartheid, I struck up an acquaintanceship with Robinson. He was approachable and responsive to intelligent questions. The Dodgers and the then Boston Braves barnstormed north in late March, playing a game a day in different locales. Florida, Alabama, Mississippi, Louisiana—traveling every night by Pullman cars in roomettes, sort of rolling studio apartments that included a foldaway bed and a sink. On a train chugging north toward Tennessee, I sought out Robinson in his. We sat facing each other, knees almost touching. "I just want you to know, Jack, that I think this racist stuff is disgraceful."

He met my gaze calmly and made a brief answer. "Then write it."

When racist episodes erupted, I reported on them. Sometimes, my stories were killed. Hard as this may be to realize in the twenty-first century, at least two prominent editors at the so-called "liberal Republican" *Trib* did not believe blacks belonged in big-league baseball. "We will not be Jackie Robinson's sounding board," the chief of the sports copy desk told me in an angry wire. But newspapering is an inexact science, and some of my pieces split the Cotton Curtain on Forty-First Street. St. Louis players shouting at Robinson, "Hey, porter, grab my bag!" Some in the Cincinnati dugout holding up spiked shoes and calling, "Shine these, will ya, Jack?" From the Philadelphia dugout, "You can't play ball up here. You're just in there to bring in nigger bucks." Nobody else back then was even trying to cover such stuff. Simply by doing what seemed fair and right—shining a spotlight on vituperation—I drew more than my share of exclusive stories.

In the late winter of 1953 Robinson hired me to help him start *Our Sports,* a monthly magazine planned for a black audience. "All the activities of Negroes in sports in one interpretive medium for the vast Negro audience," a promotional brochure promised. Would I write a bylined article in alternate issues and help Robinson prepare his own column, which would appear every month? "I can only get you $150—that's $150 a month, not a week," Robinson said. "I wish it could be more. But I'd like to work with you, and I hope you'd like to work with me."

I remember my acceptance speech verbatim. "That would be great, Jack." And it was. Meeting in hotel rooms and Pullman cars and coffee shops, we formed a splendid intimacy, which was not without moments of civil but distinct disagreement. Supposedly the theme of our pieces was baseball, but as we traveled the country sharing the intensity of both a pennant race and journalism, we touched on money, lust, and diverse aspects of the human condition.

The mainstream white press in the 1950s was ignoring the racism that lay about. As Jackie and I talked we found ourselves bursting with story ideas.

Would there ever be a black manager in the major leagues? We hoped so and suggested as candidates Campanella and Monte Irvin, the splendid Giants' outfielder. Neither became a manager, and it was twenty-three years before the Cleveland Indians broke that line by putting Frank Robinson in charge.

Why were blacks barred from being jockeys? They could be exercise boys, but they were never hired to ride races. (The systematic exclusion of black riders continued through most of the twentieth century.)

Didn't Satchel Paige belong in the then all-white Hall of Fame? Of course he did, but it was eighteen more years before Satch made it.

Was the New York Yankees' organization bigoted? Jack felt certain the answer was yes. The Yankees had dealt away the late Vic Power, a gifted black Puerto Rican first baseman, because, some Yankee executives told newspapermen as background, "The guy isn't right for us. He likes white women." Heaven forfend! I like white women myself. Power would bat .319 for the A's in 1955.

Jackie's own columns did not shy from controversy. He laced one of praise for Branch Rickey, the man who signed him, with a few small arrows aimed at O'Malley, who forced Rickey out of Brooklyn. He discussed his feud with Leo Durocher, then managing the Giants, and said that from his point of view the feud was over. Durocher responded with a letter saying he would be proud to have Jack as a friend.

The black reading public and many whites swamped us with mail, but the mainstream press, almost entirely white and male, ignored our stories. That hurt, and the economics of American journalism also worked against us. To survive, we needed ads from Campbell's Soup and General Motors, rich red tomato soup, Chevrolet convertibles painted in a pale green color called "honeydew." But the advertising never came.

Robinson told me in a hotel room in Pittsburgh that the future looked grim, and he had now better put his name to a story on his baseball legacy. "My goal has been this," he said. "That all ballplayers, regardless of race, creed or color, be accepted as ballplayers only and that they be judged simply on the basis of their ability.

"When one or two of the Cardinals shouted porter and shoeshine boy at me, I was steamed but not insulted. If a great many Negroes have to earn a living as porters and shoeshine boys, the fault for the most part is not with the Negroes themselves."

He singled out several teammates for praise: Carl Erskine, Gil Hodges, Pee Wee Reese. "But my own goal has not been achieved. I hoped to become just another ballplayer. I'm not. I don't suppose I ever will be. But in time that day will come. For now all of us must work and fight to bring it closer."

Our Sports folded after just five issues, on a day when the Dodgers defeated the Chicago Cubs. In the locker room afterward, Jackie said, "Did you get paid?"

"All but the last $150."

"Where are you going?"

"Home, I guess."

"You're coming with me."

Jack drove us to the offices of *Our Sports* and stood over the publisher and glared. I settled for $120. Next day, Robinson took me into a clothing store in which he had an interest and commandeered $30 worth of shirts, which he presented to me.

Looking back on the high deeds of Jackie Robinson, I remember a man of courage and integrity. O'Malley tried to trade him to the Giants—sacrilege in Brooklyn—and wrote a fatuous letter:

*I do know how you and your youngsters must have felt. It was a sad
day for us as well. The roads of life have a habit of recrossing. There
could well be a future intersection. Until then, my best. Au revoir.*

"If it makes him so sad," Robinson said, showing me the letter, "why
did the son of a bitch trade me in the first place?" Robinson then retired from baseball, after selling the announcement to *Look* magazine
for $50,000.

That was after the season of 1956. From that year until Jack died,
in the autumn of 1972, Major League Baseball, which now celebrates
him annually, never offered him a job. Not as a coach. Not as a manager. Not as a general manager. Not as commissioner. That would have
been something rich and strange. Jack Roosevelt Robinson, Commissioner of Baseball. Instead baseball gave us Bowie Kuhn, whose law
firm later went bankrupt, and General William Eckert, who came and
went as the unknown soldier.

In his later years a combination of high blood pressure and diabetes
wasted Robinson's great athletic body. In time he walked with a limp
and went virtually blind. Before the 1972 All-Star Game, a fan soft-
tossed a baseball to him for an autograph. The ball struck him on the
forehead. He could not see it.

But even in infirmity, he never complained. Red Smith was won-
derfully right when he described Jack as "the unconquerable."

I remember these things, and I remember, too, what Jackie did after
Our Sports folded its tent. Taking a long look back, I have to say that
when Jackie died, I lost more than an irreplaceable friend. I also lost
the best collection agent I ever had.

Victor Felipe				
Pellot Pové (Power)	◇	◇	◇	
ESMERALDA SANTIAGO				

I became a sports fan in college, when a boyfriend insisted that the only way we could be together was if I shared his favorite pastime: cheering for Boston teams. I spent countless miserable hours in the freezing cold at Schaefer Stadium in Foxborough, screaming for the New England Patriots. Too many evenings in smelly Boston Garden with the Bruins and the Celtics made me question my attachment to the boyfriend. I disliked the violence of armored men crashing against one another on ice, or the frantic back-and-forth of too-tall men with knobby knees running from one end of a floor to the other, yelling and pointing as they chased a dribbling ball. In the spring I was practically dragged to a game in Fenway Park. High above third base as the sun set, I fell in love with baseball—a relationship that outlasted the boyfriend.

It's the romance of the game that captivates me, the slow pace, the fact that it's a team sport in which every individual has his own spot and his own spotlight. I also love the pastoral language of park, fields, and mounds. And as George Carlin so hilariously explained, the object is to arrive home safely, something everyone can identify with. In

Spanish, baseball is even more romantic. The field is a *jardín*, a garden, and the base is a *cojín*, a cushion.

Whether in English or Spanish, sexual innuendo abounds in baseball—or maybe it's just me. The players are young men, plying their trade at the pinnacle of their strength and agility. They wear tight uniforms that display thigh muscles, sculpted buttocks, broad backs, muscled chests, six-pack abdomens. Well, okay, we can't see the chest muscles or the abs, but we know they're there. I nearly swooned when I saw the image of Jim Palmer in his Jockey briefs on an enormous billboard over Times Square in the late 1970s.

Admittedly, I have always objectified *peloteros* in the same way some men drool over Pamela Anderson or the latest soft-core starlets. My favorites are eye candy. If they have Hall of Fame numbers, all the better, but I'm a fan more enthralled by the beauty of the game and its players than by statistics. In 1994, however, I met a *pelotero* and was reminded that beyond their physical prowess and percentages, they are real men with histories.

I was visiting Cleveland and was invited to a reception at the home of a local judge. Inside the Victorian-style home, men and women in tailored suits were chatting and exchanging business cards with abandon. In the center of the parlor was a tall black man wearing an orange-on-orange patterned long-sleeved shirt and a flowery tie, brown pants, good leather shoes. He was bald, in his early sixties, I guessed, and exuded pride and self-confidence but also an openness that invited people closer. He was surrounded, and I soon lost sight of him as my host introduced me to bankers and politicians and his wife gave me a tour of their renovated home. As I admired the upstairs rooms, my attention often returned to the parlor, where a deep voice exclaimed, "Oh, baby!" followed by rumbling laughter. Somehow, I knew that the voice and the phrase belonged to the man with the orange shirt.

By the time I made it to the front of the house, my escort tugged me toward the door. I was scheduled to deliver a lecture at a university in less than an hour, and she fretted that we were running late, but as we stepped outside, the man with the orange shirt and the booming voice stopped me.

"You're not leaving already?" he asked in accented English. He was clean-shaven and smelled like a man who spent time on his appearance, especially if he was to meet ladies. His onyx eyes crinkled merrily. His hand was large and soft, warm, and he squeezed mine ever so gently as he introduced himself as Vic Power. When his name was unfamiliar to me, he switched to Spanish. *"En Puerto Rico soy Victor Pellot."*

"Lo siento. I haven't lived in Puerto Rico for years," I muttered in my defense.

When he realized that his name didn't ring a bell in English or in Spanish, a rueful smile crossed his features.

"Don't worry," he said. "You were probably a baby when I had my best season." He laughed generously, and I understood that he had faced greater disappointments than my ignorance.

My escort reminded me that we had to go.

"Un momentito," Vic said. "They told me you're an author, and I want to tell you something, in case you ever want to write about a baseball player."

People constantly offer their lives to writers, usually prefaced by regrets that they are not "creative" or lack discipline, the reason why, they believe, their life stories are not best-sellers. But Vic did not apologize for not writing. His voice settled into its lowest registers, and he spoke quickly in Spanish.

"I should have been the first black man to play for the Yankees," he said.

Someone emerged from the house, so Vic guided me away to the corner of the porch, where we would not be in the way as other guests departed.

"As you know, on the island we're all mixed together, black and white and brown, and no one cares. Here," he continued, "black and dark Latino players suffer a lot, even now. But when I was playing, it was worse. I couldn't travel in the same bus with my white teammates, couldn't stay in the same hotels. The white fans insulted me, the managers yelled ugly names. The umpires called balls as strikes. The coaches told the pitchers to throw at my head. The reporters said my playing was too flashy. I had my own style, you see, but they thought I was showing off."

His voice rose and fell with such emotion that I was riveted. A few feet away, my escort clicked her heels against the pavement so that I could hear her anxiety, but she was too polite to interrupt.

"It was terrible," he continued, "but it was worse when I went back to Puerto Rico. They said I changed my name to English so that the fans here would accept me. But the name was changed before I was even born by an American teacher who didn't think my mother's last name sounded right. . . . It was Pové, and the teacher made it Power. I've never renounced being Puerto Rican. I've always been proud of who I am and where I came from."

I didn't know this man, but I responded to the passion behind his words. Under the dim porch light, I couldn't see his features except for infrequent flashes from his eyes. The same voice that had rebounded through the overstuffed rooms on the other side of the wall had a completely different quality here. It was soft, but there was controlled anger behind his tone, behind his words.

"I'm telling you all this," he said, "so you can put it in one of your books."

"*Gracias*, I appreciate it," I said, "but my books are about my life and my own experiences."

"I know," he said. "Me and you, talking here today, that's an experience." He laughed again, and the intensity of the last few minutes melted away, as if whatever pain he'd felt as he was talking could only disappear with a joke. But we both knew that none of it was funny.

He took my elbow and led me down the porch steps to the sidewalk and opened the car door. He was courtly in an old-fashioned way, a man who enjoyed making a woman feel like a princess. When he was a young man, I thought, women must have flocked to him. I learned later that he was older than he looked, sixty-eight when we met in 1994, but there was something still seductive and romantic about him that kept me wondering about him for years. His story and his struggle stayed with me, and as soon as I returned home to New York, I searched for more information about him.

Victor Felipe Pellot Pové (Power) was a baseball legend. The right-hander revolutionized first base by using only his glove rather than both hands, as everyone was expected to do then, a move that gained him more flexibility and an extra stretch. He made his teammates nervous by positioning himself so far from his base that they had to learn to throw the ball where he should be and hope he'd get there on time to catch it. He did. At the plate, he tipped his bat to the ground then swung it back and forth like a pendulum. Pitchers thought that he liked the ball low, so they threw at eye level and were stunned at how quickly his bat rose to connect.

He was a star in the Caribbean leagues, and was picked up by the Yankees organization, but despite good numbers and devoted fans, he was not sent to The Big Show. According to journalists, who considered him the top Yankees' prospect, Vic was too flamboyant for the staid, conservative management. His penchant for light-skinned women, big cars, and colorful clothes made them nervous. To the dismay of his New York fans, he was traded to the hapless Philadelphia A's before the 1955 season. Elston Howard, one of his teammates in the minors, was moved up to become the first black to play for the Yankees. Vic, however, was the first black Puerto Rican to play in the major leagues and the first Puerto Rican to be picked as an All-Star (1955). He stayed with the A's when they moved to Kansas City but was traded to the Cleveland Indians after his third season. In a storied game in 1958, the Indians were trailing the Detroit Tigers. Vic tied the game in the eighth inning by stealing home, then did it again in the tenth. Cleveland won.

Vic was a charismatic, exciting player with balletic grace and dramatic flair. Over the course of fifteen seasons with six teams, he was selected as an All-Star seven times and won seven Gold Gloves. He never achieved the kind of numbers to ensure enshrinement in the Hall of Fame, but his electrifying play on the field and his struggles away from it were the source of countless stories and anecdotes. His one-liners were legendary, almost always in response to the bigotry and prejudice he endured as a black man in a racist society.

As a child, Vic had loved to draw and paint, and considered becoming an artist. As an adult, he haunted museums in the cities where he played, sought out live jazz and classical music performances, enjoyed fine restaurants, big cars, blondes. After retirement from the major leagues, he returned to Puerto Rico, where he became a respected, beloved mentor to a generation of players. He was a coach, a teacher, a manager, and a raconteur. He features prominently in David Maraniss's biography of Roberto Clemente, and appears in Dan Klores's documentary *Viva Baseball* reminiscing about the challenges he and other Latino players faced in the big leagues. By the time of the interview for the film, he was riddled with the cancer that would claim his life some months later, in November 2005.

I wish I had seen Victor Felipe Pellot Pové (Power) running the bases, or reaching for a grounder, or catching a foul ball one-handed when no one did it that way, then flicking his glove as if saying, "You didn't think I could do it, did you?" Many who did see him play insist that he was the best first baseman who has ever covered that position. I'm not so lucky, but I cherish the few moments long past his playing days when we stood together on that October evening on a Victorian porch in Cleveland, a city where neither of us lived. He gave me the biggest gift a writer can receive, a good story. It's taken all these years to put it in a book, Vic, but here it is. *Gracias.*

Michael Jordan
SEAN MANNING

Michael Jordan played one season with the Chicago White Sox AA affiliate Birmingham Barons. He batted .202 with three home runs. He had twenty-six more strikeouts than hits. He led the team in caught stealing and errors among outfielders, and was spared being last in slugging percentage thanks only to a rarely used utility man who went ofer in eleven plate appearances. He is my all-time favorite baseball player. No, this is not a put-on—although that's sort of how it began.

My real favorite, ever since I was a kid, had been San Diego Padres' Hall of Fame right fielder and eight-time National League batting champ Tony Gwynn. But who'd want to read a two-thousand-plus-word panegyric to proper swing mechanics? And for those few who might, they'd be much better served perusing Ted Williams's *The Science of Hitting* or Charley Lau's *The Art of Hitting .300* or Gwynn's own *The Art of Hitting* than any insights on the subject I—a seven-hole staple throughout most of high school and summer ball whose penchant for going the other way was owed not to the emulation of my idol but to criminally slow bat speed—might offer.

Instead, and particularly in light of the Cleveland Cavaliers' recent ousting from the NBA playoffs at the hands of the underdog Orlando Magic, I had the idea to write of Jordan: of how when I was growing up in northeastern Ohio in the late '80s and early '90s—the reason Gwynn was my favorite, short on boyhood hero material as were the atrocious Indians clubs of that period—he'd been my sworn enemy, the bane of my existence for leading his Chicago Bulls past the Cavs in no less than four postseasons; and of how he was my favorite base-ball player because upon retiring from basketball in the fall of 1993 in order to pursue the sport, he gave the Cavs the chance to win their first championship ever.

Except they didn't. By just past the midway point of that 1993–1994 season, two of the Cavs' starters, five-time All-Star center Brad Daugh-erty and three-time All-Star forward Larry Nance, had sustained year-ending—and ultimately career-ending—injuries. Cleveland still somehow managed to finish a respectable twelve games over .500 and earn a playoff spot but was swept in the first round (by, yup, Chicago). And then, of course, in the latter half of the following season, Jordan issued his famously terse press release—"I'm back"—quit baseball, and returned to the Bulls, thereby slamming shut the Cavs' window of opportunity. So the whole His Airness–as-favorite-player hornswoggle didn't really work.

And yet the more I thought about it . . .

Daugherty would play his last game on February 23, 1994, Nance on March 12. Bitter and contemptuous as I was feeling, knowing that with those two gone so were the Cavs' title hopes, nothing could've cheered me more than the sight of that March 14 *Sports Illustrated* cover: Jordan in a White Sox spring training uniform, flailing at a pitch in some exhibition game; the ball a blur as it whizzes past; his helmet looking like it's about to topple off, the bat like it might go flying into the stands; that sinuous, Vitruvian body so intimidating in shorts and a tank top rendered laughably gawky and gangly by the pants and long sleeves beneath his jersey; on his face, an unfamiliar look of bewilderment and frustration; and, even better than the photo, in big, yellow letters the caption "Bag It, Michael!" In fact, behind only receiving Nintendo the first Christmas it came out, vacationing at Disney World, French kissing Becky Carroll in Alice Pearson's backyard, and seeing *Die Hard* in the theater, that issue of *Sports Illustrated* provided my greatest source of pleasure during childhood and early adolescence.

Reflecting on this fills me with amusement and wonder. Not at how riled up and bent out of shape by sports I'd once been able to get. I *wish* that were the case—wish I haven't been walking around these last few weeks since the Magic dumped the Cavs as sullen as after those playoff exits to the Bulls some twenty years ago. No, what humors and amazes me is that I could be so insensitive to the reason behind Jordan's career change. But then, I was fourteen. When it came to *that*, I was supposed to be incapable of empathy.

What was *Sports Illustrated*'s excuse? In response to the cover and accompanying story, Jordan vowed to boycott any future involvement with the magazine, and according to a reappraisal of his "experiment" published this past spring on *SI*'s Web site in commemoration of the fifteenth anniversary—one of two, both favorable yet nearly as repugnant as the original article for implying a belief on the part of its publishers that anything short of a wholesale retraction might be adequate expiation—has to this day kept his word. I don't blame him. I lately ordered a copy of the issue off eBay and reading the piece again found myself so indignant I could barely finish—and the second I did, hurled the damn thing across the room:

> *Shame on* [the White Sox] *for their cynical manipulation of the public. And shame on them for feeding Michael's matchbook-cover delusion—* BECOME A MAJOR LEAGUER IN JUST SIX WEEKS!

*Next to his name and vital statistics on the official list of 1994
White Sox, where his '93 batting stats should be, it reads DID NOT
PLAY. It should read HASN'T PLAYED IN 15 YEARS!*

As Jordan long-tossed with centerfielder Lance Johnson [during
Chicago's first spring training game], *the White Sox staged some
sort of promotional stunt along the third baseline: Two fans had to
race each other after running around a bat ten times. It was hard to
tell which gimmick was more ridiculous, the one down by third or the
one in right.*

Jordan [in his first spring training at bat] *swung . . . and, befit-
ting a great basketball player, he hit a dribbler down the first base
line. One small dribbler for a man, one giant dribbler for mankind.*

What makes the article all the more abhorrent—that is, in addition
to the *Sports Illustrated* Store advertisement later in the magazine for
"The Michael Jordan Thrill Pack": two VHS tapes of Jordan highlights
and a special issue commemorating his and the Bulls' three consecutive titles ($39.90 plus $4.95 shipping and handling)—is another one
a few pages later detailing the comeback attempts of Darryl Strawberry
and Jose Canseco, with the Los Angeles Dodgers and Texas Rangers,
respectively. Hampered by injury the previous couple of seasons, the
former superstar sluggers had in that time become better known for
their off-field exploits. Strawberry admitted to being suicidal, was arrested for allegedly assaulting his girlfriend, came under federal investigation for tax evasion, and remarked during a spell of L.A. wildfires,
"Let it burn." Canseco, arrested in 1989 for illegal possession of a
firearm, was involved in a prolonged and messy public divorce from
his first wife and taken into police custody after ramming his Porsche
into her BMW early one morning outside a Miami nightclub. Though

it acknowledges most of these offenses, however, the piece is overall complimentary:

> *The best thing about life is you get lots of at bats; you can make up for anything.*

> *... there is nothing more American than a comeback.*

> *His hitting and legs, Canseco believes, are 100%; his arm is perhaps 70%. But more significantly, his heart and head are also healing ahead of schedule.*

Canseco's heart and head? What of Jordan's? Not once in *SI*'s hatchet job is his father mentioned.

If you're unaware of the circumstances surrounding the July 1993 murder of James Jordan, just as I defer to Williams's, Lau's, and Gwynn's treatises with regard to the intricacies of hitting, so do I here to "Reasonable Doubt," Scott Raab's exhaustive, *In Cold Blood*–esque examination of the homicide and ensuing investigation for the March 1994 issue of *Esquire*. By then, by the time Jordan entered White Sox camp in Sarasota, what little magnanimity the press had shown in its coverage of the tragedy—few initial reports that I could find resisted inviting the possibility that it was connected to recent revelations of MJ's high-stakes gambling habit—had all but dissipated. *SI* was hardly the only outlet disparaging of the then three-time NBA regular season and Finals MVP's shift from court to diamond. That spring and summer, the *New York Times* ran roughly twenty stories' worth of coverage—"Swish Just Won't Cut It in Jordan's New Sport," "Jordan at Break: .194, 78 Strikeouts," and "Fences Undented as Jordan Swings Away" just a few of the headings. The *Times*'s hostility is not entirely surprising given that after the Cavs, the team Jordan seemed to most relish making his bitch was the Knicks. But even his hometown *Chicago Tribune* couldn't abstain: "About This Jordan Nonsense," "A 'No' to Michael," "Experts Evaluate Jordan's Chances: Just Forget About It," "Time to Catch Up, Cubs: It's Your Turn to Send in a Clown." Still less cordial to the idea were, for the most part, major leaguers themselves. "He had better tie his Air Jordans real tight if I pitch to him," Randy Johnson, then of the Seattle Mariners, was quoted by *SI* as saying. "I'd like to see how much air time he'd get on one of my inside pitches."

It's so easy now to ridicule those bozos and their objections—what with all that's happened to baseball in the decade and a half since—it's not even fun.

They said he was an embarrassment to the game. Yeah, next to PEDs and $1,000+ ticket-gouging and four-month holdouts for $45 million two-year deals, not so much. (Although White Sox and Bulls' owner Jerry Reinsdorf pledged to honor Jordan's basketball contract for the year—$4 million—Jordan, by all accounts, hadn't insisted or even asked and was paid just $850 a month plus $16 a day meal money in the minors. And while he *did* insist on a new luxury bus for team travel and helped with the financing, this wasn't him acting the prima donna, as opined by most of the media, but rather, according to a rare charitable *Times* article, him being afraid after what had happened to his father that the old bus might break down and strand them on some dark and deserted road.)

They said he'd be depriving more deserving players of the roster spot, possibly even cutting short their careers. Had he made the big-league squad, Jordan would've replaced either outfielder Mike Huff or Warren Newson, a loss from which—in either case—*SI* seemed to suggest the national pastime might never recover . . . Huff was dealt just before Opening Day to Toronto for an infielder who spent the entire season with the White Sox Triple-A club, while Newson hit just .255

in all of sixty-three games and the following year was traded to Seattle. Charles Poe, the guy demoted to make room on the Barons, would get back to Birmingham in 1995, when he made the Southern League All-Star team; he'd eventually advance as far as Triple-A in both the Padres' and Oakland Athletics' organizations but was never called up.

They said with his Nike batting gloves and high-top spikes, his Wilson wristbands and mitt, the Gatorade bottle he was seen swigging from in the dugout so often it seemed fused to his hand, he was nothing but a human billboard, a shameless marketing device. On this point, at least, they weren't wholly incorrect. Going so far as to drape an American flag over his shoulder during the 1992 Olympic basketball medal ceremony and thus conceal the team warm-up's Reebok logo, Jordan was as shrewd and loyal a corporate spokesperson as there's ever been in pro sports, as there's ever been, period. (And he remains so—requiring a patch be sewn over the Reebok logo on a Chicago Blackhawks hockey jersey he wore for an appearance at one of the team's 2009 playoff games.) In 1994, he'd earn an estimated $30 million from endorsements, and naturally *SI* was quick to note the Nike merchandise van raking it in from its post outside the Florida stadium. Yet Jordan's shilling was scrupulous compared with Major League Baseball's current *seventy-plus* official sponsors, with Target Field, Citi Field, Chase Field, Progressive Field, U.S. Cellular Field, Citizens Bank Park, Comerica Park, AT&T Park, PNC Park, Minute Maid Park. . . .

But it's what they *didn't* say, the reason for all the outrage that, as far as I'm aware, *wasn't* articulated, that more interests me.

"The wisdom of life," maintains Marlow in *Lord Jim*, "consists in putting out of sight all the reminders of our folly, of our weakness, of our mortality; all that makes against our efficiency—the memory of our failures, the hints of our undying fears, the bodies of our dead friends." This is where sport comes in. It's order to life's chaos, perpetual youth and vigor to life's aging and infirmity. It's diversion, distraction, escape. We don't watch it to be reminded of our physical and emotional frailties—in other words, our humanity. Had Jordan remained in basketball and dedicated that 1993–1994 season to the memory of his father, committed to win a fourth straight title in his honor, you can bet there'd have flowed from all corners an outpouring of unconditional support and nary an ill word written or said of him. Because—as had been Notre Dame's "Win One for the Gipper" upset of Army in 1928 and Bo Kimble's left-handed free throws in tribute to departed friend and teammate Hank Gathers during eleventh-seeded Loyola Marymount's uncanny run to the Elite Eight round of the 1990 NCAA tournament, as would be Brett Favre's four first-half touchdowns that 2003 Monday night in Oakland a mere twenty-four hours after his own father's unexpected passing—that would have been keeping consistent with the accepted narrative of sport. Retiring and taking up baseball (James Jordan always held his son had shown sufficient promise in Little League and high school to one day play professionally, and had been encouraging him to try doing so since 1990, even before the first Bulls championship) was not. It flipped the script, was instead a clear indication of just how difficult a time he was having with his father's death. And if *Michael Jordan* had trouble handling the loss of one of his parents, what did that foretell for everyone else, all the non-Übermensches? How unraveled could they anticipate coming when their own went? People didn't appreciate being made to think about this, didn't like how real shit had gotten, and so they lashed out. As for those who did so, who'd already lost one or both parents, they were simply jealous, for how much they'd have loved to have been able to quit their jobs and go play ball and horse around with the guys and just not be a grown-up for a while.

I know I would've. It's going on two years since my mom died. She was fifty-nine, three years older than James Jordan. I was twenty-eight, two years younger than MJ. (As long as he'd been in the NBA and as much as he'd accomplished, it's easy to forget he was only thirty when his father was killed.) I haven't dealt with it well, either—pushed my girlfriend away, distanced myself from family and friends. I'm finally starting to come to terms with it, but it's still a struggle, every day is, and not an hour goes by when I don't think of her. So that's how Michael Jordan came to supplant Tony Gwynn as my favorite. Gwynn aspired to winning a World Series, reaching 3,000 hits, making a serious run at .400. Jordan just missed his dad. I can't think of a better reason to play the game than that.

Garry Maddox
DOUG GLANVILLE

With each increasing helmet size, he seemed to get better. I never really understood the power of the 'fro until I challenged myself to let my hair grow in a futile attempt to catch him. But Garry Lee Maddox, a.k.a. the Secretary of Defense, one of my childhood favorite players, would ultimately prevail in the competition for hair dominance.

I would never catch him in hair, and I would never catch him in championship rings, but I did have tenure in Philadelphia as a member of the same organization he helped win the World Series in 1980. Through my years as a Phillie, I had a chance to spend a lot of time with Garry. It was surreal. For many years I followed the Phillies as a young fan in Teaneck, New Jersey. I followed their box scores religiously, and would simulate their seasons with my handy Strat-O-Matic baseball set or my Wiffle ball bat. Like clockwork, I would pick the Phillies in my brother's "Strat" leagues, and Maddox would patrol center.

One of the thrills of rising in the minor leagues is that all along the way you meet your childhood icons in the flesh. My coaches were a litany of former major leaguers, previously real only on a baseball card or a TV set. All of a sudden, Billy Williams was teaching me how to hit; Jimmy Piersall was showing me how to cut off a ball in the gap; and Garry Maddox was sharing how to position myself in the hallowed vastness of Veterans Stadium's center field, though his point of emphasis was more about how to prepare for the baseball afterlife.

What struck me instantly about Garry was that he had a genuine concern for the next generation of baseball players. There was none of the tension that sometimes rears its head over the spoils of today's game having been built on the backs and sacrifices of the generation beforehand. He was open and available to mentor young players, and I was fortunate to be one of the biggest recipients of his advice.

This might come as a surprise from someone who signed a six-year contract with the Phillies after their World Championship season only to lose his starting job three years into it. But he understood that time is ticking on every player, and that most are completely unprepared for the life after the game. The vast majority don't have a résumé, nor have they experienced many job interviews that didn't involve a bat or a ball. However, some are more willing to adapt than others, and the world of business is ripe for people who are used to competing. After refusing to waive a no-trade clause, Garry just adroitly bided his time, and by the end of his contract (and basically his career), he was enrolled full-time at Temple University. He spent time on the road trips cultivating his business network as much as he did his swing.

He diligently purchased an office furniture business named A. Pomerantz and Company, founded at the tail end of the nineteenth century. After taking some hard lumps—caused in part, he explained, by the naïve thought that he could just direct the pre-existing team by sheer inspiration—he hit his stride, turning it into a successful business that supplies office furniture to many key corporations in the Philadelphia market. As he told me, "You have to be willing to learn the easy way by knowing who you can trust and who to put in the right place." Loyalty is a big part of who he is, and not just because he is grateful and values relationships but because he understands that it can be good for any endeavor you can dream of pursuing. Relationships allow you to have a foundation steeped in trust.

When I told him after the 2002 season that I was going to sign with the Texas Rangers, he took me out to a networking party where I met some of the most notable people in Philadelphia, a city where he had lived for close to three decades, a city that he still had in the palm of his hand. He didn't tell me to stay in Philly, but he showed me that there was a lot of love and respect for me in the city. He contended that this was worth something that couldn't be matched by the Rangers' promise to give me a shot at being the starting center fielder.

Despite his compelling argument, I did leave for Texas. He was disappointed, but he understood. The year before, I had lost my father on the last day of the season, and I needed a new home, a getaway year to get back to form. Still, I always carried with me Garry's point: It is about relationships.

It was during my time with the Rangers that I let my hair grow to record proportions. My usual 7 3/8 helmet size rose to a size 8 with afro puffs sticking out of every hole in the helmet. I was away from the Philadelphia nest built on five years of major-league time and four years of college. It felt liberating, and the hair expressed this with all its wonder.

By the next season, I was back with the Phillies, a year older, a year wiser, and more primed than ever to listen to what the Secretary had to dictate, personally as well as professionally. Garry had helped me find the strength to get out of a previous relationship. He was tactical; in contrast to his cool demeanor, he had a relentless approach that quietly snuck up on an unsuspecting target. And he seemed to end up in a strong position even if it took a long time to get there. "You are accepting less by giving her excuses," he had said. Closing that door opened up the one that led to the woman who would become my wife, but Garry would use his Socratic method in conversation about her (or more on "the concept of marriage") as well.

"As we are sitting here at this dinner table and a group of young ladies wants to sit down and talk to you," he'd ask, "would it be appropriate to let them if you are married?" Then he would let you go into all these scenarios to explain yourself, only to give you the right answer after you went in circles for minutes, if not hours. He wanted you to figure out the right question to ask and then answer it with conviction. If he got that, he had done his job. Despite his third-degree grilling, when I looked up on my wedding day, there was Garry in full support.

He attended just about every event to which he was invited. A group of my teammates and I got involved in Philadelphia Futures, a wonderful charity that provides mentors to talented students to help them sustain their studies. We set up an annual fund-raiser, a celebrity and sponsor-driven pool tournament. Garry took his cue shot year in and year out. He held a fund-raiser of his own every off-season, a bowling event for a golf academy for at-risk youth. He'd sell out every lane with celebrity bowlers and sponsors. Every year it seemed like the entire city of Philly was at the event, nicely fitting in the palm of his Gold-Gloved hand.

My own time as a major leaguer was coming to a close, and after getting released by the Yankees in 2005, I sat down with my future wife and plotted out the next steps. Since both of us were transitioning out of a major job, we decided to make a move to Chicago, the city in which I started my big-league career, which I have always held in high regard.

After settling there, I made a trip back to Philadelphia for a charity event arranged by a friend from high school. I talked to Garry, and he agreed to attend and sign autographs with me in a booth for a couple of hours. He had tremendous charisma with fans and an uncanny ability to be accessible, and everyone walked away feeling as if Garry Maddox had known them for years. But all along and in between signings, he spoke to me about my future. He expressed an almost fatherly disappointment in my entrenchment in a difficult real estate business, which in some ways paralleled his trying times early in his entrepreneurial career. He felt I could have been further along in the business of the game, positioned to be a GM or a key cog in the commissioner's office. But I was building homes.

By the time the session was over, I'd decided to revamp my life plan. I would build on some baseball relationships to reconnect with the game, but from a different kind of angle: from the perspective of a writer.

"Two-thirds of the earth is covered by water; the other third is covered by Garry Maddox," was the line coined by legendary broadcasters who watched him play. We know about his exceptional ability to be a captain of the outfield, how he was always a step ahead of his opponents, knew something they did not, made it seem like he was teleporting between spots, not just gliding his way to record another out. He moves with similar precision in his conversations, and whenever you need him he is there in a flash, as if he was cutting a ball off in the gap. His grace on the field matches how he carries himself off it, and he's been as influential in shaping who I want to be as a person as he was in shaping who I wanted to be as a ballplayer.

Joe Morgan wrote in his book *A Life in Baseball* about the experience of developing his relationship with Coca-Cola to test the entrepreneurial waters. He encouraged Garry to think ahead, but he also impressed upon him the importance of mentoring the next young Garry Maddox. As Joe put it, "Maybe you can help show someone else the way now."

In my days with the Phillies, the local press constantly compared my outfield play to Garry's. I could not accept such a comparison. It's one thing to surpass your teacher, but you cannot surpass a legend in your own mind. Even if you can outdo his 'do.

Yutaka Enatsu
ROBERT WHITING

Not much is known in North America about Yutaka Enatsu, a southpaw who was perhaps the best pitcher who ever played the game in Japan. But those Americans who had the chance to see him certainly never forgot the experience.

Red Schoendienst, who watched Enatsu dominate his touring St. Louis Cardinals in a goodwill exhibition game in 1968, said, "He is one of the best left-handed pitchers I have ever seen. He could teach Steve Carlton a thing or two." Said former Yankee Clete Boyer, who batted against Enatsu while playing for the Taiyo Whales from 1972 to 1975, "He was something else. At his best, he was as good as anyone I ever faced and that includes Bob Gibson. His fastball literally exploded at you." Jim Lefebvre, an ex-Dodger who also played in Japan during that era, compared him to Sandy Koufax.

Had Enatsu played at a time when there was free agency in Japan and when selling one's baseball talents to Major League Baseball was not considered an act of national betrayal, he would have unquestionably been a star in the United States. He might also have wound up in a federal prison—but more on that later.

Enatsu was born in 1948 and grew up in the Minami, the entertainment section of Osaka—a tough, dense thicket of bars, nightclubs, and restaurants. After being kicked off his junior high school team for fighting, he refocused his energies and went on to become a standout pitcher for Osaka Gakuin High School. Drafted Number 1 by Hanshin at nineteen, he led all of Japanese professional baseball in strikeouts with 225, the most ever for a rookie just out of high school, while compiling a record of 12–13 and an ERA of 2.74. And remarkably enough, he did it with only one pitch—his fastball.

In Enatsu's second year, he learned to throw a curve and took his game to a higher level. He won twenty-five games, set a single-game strikeout mark of sixteen, and broke the then single-season mark of 353 strikeouts in a way so spectacular that people still talk about it in Japan.

The Hanshin Tigers' archrival was (and still is) the Yomiuri Giants of Tokyo, the oldest, winningest team in the land, with a history dating back to 1936. (The Giants are Japan's Yankees, the Tigers its Red Sox.) Enatsu had developed a special rivalry with the Giants' legendary Taiwanese slugger Sadaharu Oh, who, at age twenty-eight, was on his way to his fifth straight home-run crown and a career total of 868; knowledgeable American observers compared him favorably to Ted Williams and Hank Aaron. Over the course of their career, no other pitcher would strike out Oh as often as Enatsu, and no other batter would hit as many home runs off Enatsu as Oh.

In mid-September, the Tigers headed into a four-game series with the Giants, the two teams locked in a fierce battle for first place. With his strikeout total at 347, Enatsu brashly announced he would break the record in game one against Oh.

The game took place at Koshien Stadium, the cavernous, antiquated home of the Tigers outside Osaka. Before a capacity crowd of 55,000 fans, in stifling, sauna-bath heat, Enatsu struck out Oh in the first inning, on an in-high fastball, and again in the fourth inning, on a 1–2 curveball that slid over the plate. It was his sixth strikeout of the game, which put him right at 353.

Back in the dugout, his uniform soaked in sweat, Enatsu declared to his teammates he would not strike out any more batters until Oh came to bat again. It was an incredible thing to say given the circumstances—a scoreless tie in a must-win game—but Enatsu was true to his word. He retired the next eight hitters in a row on infield ground balls and pop flies. Then Oh stepped in, assuming his famous one-foot-in-the-air flamingo stance. As Tigers cheerleaders furiously waved their banners and conducted deafening chants of encouragement, Enatsu whiffed him on four pitches, the last an inside ninety-five-mile-per-hour fastball at which Oh swung ferociously and missed.

That game, won by the Tigers 1–0 in the twelfth inning—on a single by Enatsu, incidentally—has been the subject of numerous magazine stories and TV documentaries over the years. A day later, in the type of iron-man performance that was becoming typical of him, Enatsu was back on the mound, pitching a four-hit shutout and fanning ten. His pitching kept the Tigers in the thick of the pennant fight until the final Giant-Tiger game of the season, a ten-inning contest that Enatsu lost by a 2–1 margin with *no* days' rest. He was voted the Sawamura Award as baseball's best pitcher after finishing with a mark of 25–12, an ERA of 2.13 and 401 strikeouts over 329 innings.

The key to Enatsu's success was near-perfect form and perfect control. Said Tiger catcher Yasuhiko Tsuji, "His curveball did not have a big break on it, but he threw everything from exactly the same motion. It was impossible to tell what pitch he was throwing. When the breaking ball did come, in the wake of his blinding fastball, it threw the batters off. He also never missed. I could put my glove anywhere, inside high, outside low, and he would always hit it dead center." (Many fans came early just to watch Enatsu play long catch in the outfield in pregame warm-ups, to see him hit his target time after time from 200 feet away.)

Enatsu would go on to win twenty games four times for Hanshin and lead the league in strikeouts four times. In time he became as famous for his off-field behavior as he was for his pitching heroics. He smoked 100 cigarettes a day and spent his nights playing pachinko and mahjong and drinking in Osaka nightclubs. With his buzz cut, he was unaffected by the longhaired counterculture youth of his time, sniffing glue in back-street coffee offices, listening to Simon and Garfunkel. He preferred socializing with *yakuza*.

Osaka was famous for its swaggering, tattooed, crew-cut gangsters, often with shorn pinkies—evidence of *yakuza*-style penance for one misdeed or another—who controlled much of the city. Enatsu, as he once confessed, had always had a thing for them. He had grown up admiring the fabled gangland credo of "*giri* and *ninjo*," duty and obligation to the gang, above all, which was based on the old samurai warrior code. When he joined the Tigers, veteran players introduced him to drinking establishments favored by gangland figures.

Movie director Kosaku Yamashita, who would cast Enatsu in a supporting role in the 1985 underworld film *Saigo no Bakuto* (*The Last Gambler*), said, "You looked at him and he acted like a gangster, a *yakuza*. He had that swagger. He really fit the part."

In 1970, the commissioner of Japanese Professional Baseball suspended Enatsu when it was discovered that he had accepted an expensive wristwatch from the boss of the powerful Takenaka-Gumi. The relevant article of the Professional Baseball Regulations was the one that prohibits "association with habitual gamblers." An investigation was launched by the commissioner's office, and two weeks later in a ruling that raised many eyebrows, it was determined that the gang boss was not really a "habitual gambler," and Enatsu was reinstated. The decision was at once evidence of how important Enatsu was to professional baseball and just how tolerant Japanese society had become of traditional *yakuza* gangs, whose front companies controlled concessions and other business at Japan's baseball stadiums, among many, many other things.

Enatsu's rebelliousness, which separated him from his compliant teammates, manifested itself in other ways. During one spring camp, in protest of the severe martial-arts-style training that Tiger pitchers were required to undergo each spring—which included throwing 3,000 pitches over a three-and-a-half-week span—he laid down in the outfield, rested his head on his glove, and went to sleep as his teammates obediently circled the field, running laps. "What's the point?" he said. "I'm going to pitch, no matter what."

The Hanshin brain trust tried in several ways to cultivate more fighting spirit. During the 1970 off-season, for example, the front office ordered him to take a part-time job in an Osaka department store to learn how to deal humbly with people. In the winter of 1971, his manager took him on a spiritual retreat to a mountain Zen temple, where he was made to rise at dawn, meditate in *seiza* fashion for seven hours a day, clean toilets, and complete other spirit-strengthening exercises. None of these efforts met a great deal of success.

In May 1971, after a series of sluggish performances, he was examined by a team physician and diagnosed with a heart condition. The doctor prescribed cortisone and other medicine, and told Enatsu that he would have to give up at least one of his four favorite activities: drinking, smoking, women, and mahjong. Enatsu thought long and hard and replied, "I can't think of life without my postgame cigarette. I'm too addicted to women and mahjong to give them up. So I guess it will have to be drinking."

Two alcohol-free months later, he started a midseason all-star game and struck out the first nine men to face him. He also hit a home run.

Enatsu pitched often on two days' rest and occasionally on one. It was something MLB coaches would never allow, but the practice was a requirement for staff aces in Japan, where the samurai spirit was a large part of the sports culture. Not surprisingly, like most other stars, he developed arm trouble and had to take painkillers in order to pitch. After he finished 23–8 in 1972 and 24–13 in 1973, the strain of so much pitching eventually caught up with him. He sank to 12–14 in 1974 and 12–12 in 1975. He lost the ability to pitch complete games, and gradually even the ability to pitch five innings. Fifty pitches was his maximum.

Unable to get along with the Tigers' new manager, Enatsu was traded to the Nankai Hawks of the Pacific League, where, after much persuasion, he agreed to become a closer—a rarity in Japan, where starting pitchers were expected to throw complete games. It was a question of pride. As Enatsu explained to a writer for a Japanese sports daily, "It's like you being transferred from the editorial department of your publication to the sales department. It's a demotion."

Having nonetheless swallowed his pride, he resurrected his career, garnering nineteen saves his first year and winning the Fireman of the Year Award, recognizing the league's most outstanding reliever, the following season. It was said he developed the ability to anticipate what the batter would do. As Masaichi Kaneda, Japan's all-time winningest pitcher, with 400 victories, put it, "Enatsu was good because he knew how to use the *Ma* [a term for a dramatic pause in Kabuki theater]. He waited for just the right moment—a lapse of concentration by the batter—to deliver the pitch. In that sense, he could really read the batter's mind."

In 1979, he was dealt back to the Central League, to the Hiroshima Carp, and won the MVP with a record of 9–5, an ERA of 2.66, and twenty-two saves. His performance in the seventh and final game of the 1979 Japan Series between the Carp and the Kintetsu Buffaloes— where he came on in the ninth to protect a one-run lead, loaded the bases, and then retired the side—is legendary in Japan. It inspired a best-selling nonfiction book entitled *21 Kyu* (*21 Pitches*).

In 1980, Enatsu helped the Carp win another Japan Series crown, but after a dispute with his manager he was traded once more to the Pacific League, to the Tokyo-based Nippon Ham Fighters, who were so desperate for a late-inning closer they were willing to surrender their ace Takahashi Naoki. In the 1981 season, after compiling an ERA of 2.82 with twenty-five saves and leading Nippon Ham to a pennant, Enatsu was named MVP—the first man to receive the honor in both leagues.

By now, Enatsu was like a masterless Ronin who traveled the land renting out his services to the lord who made the highest bid—a very fat Ronin, for he had ballooned to 220 pounds, caused, he said, by the medication he was taking.

In 1983, after leading the league in saves for the fourth year in a row, he was dealt to the Seibu Lions, in Tokorozawa, outside Tokyo. At Seibu he clashed with Lions manager Tatsuro Hirooka, a notorious disciplinarian and health food advocate. Hirooka, unhappy with Enatsu's weight and his chain smoking, among other things, dispatched him to the farm team in midseason to get in shape.

Enatsu felt so insulted he angrily left the team before the season ended and never returned (leaving a safe full of cash in his cubicle). After an unsuccessful tryout with the Milwaukee Brewers, which was heavily covered by the Japanese media, he retired.

Using just two pitches, he'd set a number of records that still stand in Japan: 401 strikeouts in one year (surpassing Sandy Koufax's American record), nine strikeouts in a row in an all-star game and fifteen in a row over three all-star contests, and an eleven-inning no-hitter (which he won by hitting a *sayonara* home run). Not to mention the fourteen-inning game he pitched during which he retired thirty-four batters in a row. All that along with his final stats—206 wins, 158 losses, an ERA of 2.49, 2,987 strikeouts in 3,196 innings pitched, only 936 walks, 193 saves (a record at the time, which was later broken by the Yokohama Bay Stars' Kazuhiro Sasaki, who went on to pitch for the Seattle Mariners)—should have made him a shoo-in for the Japanese Baseball Hall of Fame. But it was not to be.

In retirement, after undergoing heart surgery to correct his chronic condition, Enatsu found work as a television commentator and columnist for sports dailies and, in addition to his role in *The Last Gambler*, appeared in bit parts in movies and TV dramas. But there were complaints about his demands for special treatment. While visiting baseball spring camps on media assignments, for example, he insisted on being chauffeured around in a foreign car.

There were also complaints about his underworld friends, whom, according to daily newspaper *Sankei Shimbun*, he would bring to the ballpark and ensconce in the press box as well as accompany on golf excursions. Then, after his wife of nine years left him in 1984 amid accusations of infidelity, dark suspicions of drug use arose. Enatsu was occasionally seen asleep in the press box, and once, when he was several hours late to a media job, his coworkers had his hotel door pried open to find him in a deep drug-induced slumber.

On March 3, 1993, the police raided his apartment in Meguro and discovered sixteen hypodermic needles and several milligrams of a certain type of methamphetamine. Enatsu was arrested along with his girlfriend at the time. Police determined that he had received his drugs from a member of the Yamaguchi-*gumi*, Japan's largest criminal organization. The next month, at age forty-four, he was sentenced to two years and four months in prison in Shizuoka.

Prison in Japan is not an easy thing. Prisoners are intentionally deprived of heat in Japan's frigid winters and air-conditioning during its stifling summers. Talking is severely restricted, the food barely edible, baths and showers limited to once a week. More than once Enatsu was beaten for insubordination.

But some guards were former fans. They solicited autographs and allowed him to listen to baseball broadcasts on the radio. "When I climbed into the futon at night," said Enatsu, "all I thought about was baseball. I remembered all 829 games in which I pitched."

After his release, in an attempt to start with a clean slate, he threw away all his trophies. Then he tried to put his broken life back together. He married his girlfriend (his co-arrestee, who was out on probation). He appeared in old-timers games. He wrote a column in the *Daily Sports,* and in 2000 he reached a certain state of grace when two separate nationwide fan surveys named him as starting pitcher on the All-Century Japan baseball team.

More recently he has written several books, including *Enatsu No Outlaw Yakyu Ron (Enatsu's Outlaw Baseball Philosophy)* and *Message from Enatsu Yutaka to Daisuke Matsuzaka.* In them he expresses his belief that a man should "pitch until his arm falls off" and that the most important thing in sports and life is proper form. "From proper form, everything else flows."

He also writes that the way to get Ichiro out is to pitch him high and inside.

Garry Templeton
JEFF PEARLMAN

I grew up in a town where nearly everything—and everybody—was white. That was Mahopac, New York, in the 1970s and '80s: almost exclusively Caucasian, with the traditional conservative values to match. Although we were but an hour's drive from New York City, much about Mahopac oozed *Better Homes and Gardens*. Women, by and large, stayed home to cook, clean house, and care for the children. Men went off to work in their suits and ties. Everyone supported Ronald Reagan and George Bush, and whenever Willie Horton flashed across our TV screens, we instinctively shuddered while reaching for the rifles nestled gently against our stuffed elk heads.

Across the street from my house on Emerald Lane, there lived a girl who once explained to me that she would like to enjoy the music of Michael Jackson, "but his blackness makes that hard." Another neighbor—a thirteen-year-old boy—was a closet rap die-hard whose parents insisted he not wear his Run-DMC T-shirt. Heaven forbid the extended family see him. When I told my little friends that I had a crush on (pre-crack) Whitney Houston, they all agreed she was pretty—for one of "those" people. My eighth-grade history teacher, Mr. McGee, taught our class that those wacky Negroes can't ski *or*

151

swim. We had two black families living within a three-mile radius of our house. One was asked to move. The other endured two front-yard cross burnings.

And then, there were sports. In Mahopac, you rooted for the white guys, or you didn't root at all. In baseball, Mets catcher John Stearns signified hard work and endurance. In football, Giants quarterback Phil Simms stood for much of the same. When it came to the heated college basketball rivalry between St. John's and Georgetown, it was a case of good (white Chris Mullin and Lou Carnesecca) versus evil (black Patrick Ewing and John Thompson). Those chimpanzee sounds you heard whenever Ewing touched the ball? Mahopac-generated, I assure you.

This was all I knew. And while my house was one of the few liberal sanctuaries in town (both of my parents were registered Democrats and had all their teeth), it would have been easy for a young, impressionable boy to find himself sucked up in the inanity.

Thank goodness for Garry Lewis Templeton.

We met in 1981, when I was a nine-year-old fourth-grader at Lakeview Elementary. During the long days of winter, all the boys from the neighborhood would meet up in my kitchen and play "closies" with our stacks of random baseball cards. (The game was simple—everyone flips their cards toward a brick wall, and whoever's comes the closest without touching snags the entire pot.) Until that frigid November afternoon, I had never heard of Garry Templeton, the St. Louis Cardinals' shortstop. But then, upon collecting my winnings, I sorted through my deck, past Darrell Porter and Steve Kemp, past Hosken Powell and Pete O'Brien, past Omar Moreno and J.R. Richard . . . and found him.

The card in hand was a 1978 Topps, with "Cardinals" written in green script along the bottom left alongside "Garry Templeton" in black letters. What struck me was neither his stance (clearly staged for the photograph) nor his surroundings (why was he posing as a hitter outside the third-base line, sans batting helmet?) but his facial expression. It was eerily similar to the one my mother had made earlier that year when I snuck into the kitchen and ate the chocolate almond cake she had baked for my father's office party. In short, it said, "What the f%#@ is wrong with you?"

Until that moment, I had only known ballplayers to be the happy, caring, fan-friendly, family-oriented men portrayed in books like *Super Joe: The Life and Legend of Joe Charboneau* and *Steve Garvey, Storybook Star*. They smiled and laughed and loved nothing more than playing catch beneath the glorious midafternoon sun. Baseball players represented America at its finest. They were what we all aspired to become.

And yet there was Templeton with that pissed-off look on his face.

I couldn't get over the card. I just couldn't. So, in the ensuing days, I visited the Mahopac Library and started digging through old copies of *Sport* and *Sports Illustrated* and the *New York Times*. I became obsessed with all things Templeton: What sort of player was he? Why was his first name spelled with two Rs? Why was he so damned angry?

Before long, I was in love. At age twenty-five, Templeton was clearly one of the most naturally gifted shortstops the game had ever seen. His arm was compared to a rocket; his speed to Lou Brock's. In 1979 he became the first switch-hitter in baseball history to collect 100 hits from each side of the plate, and for three straight seasons he'd led the league in triples. "In all my years in baseball," Whitey Herzog, his manager, once said, "I've never seen a player with so much talent."

What really snagged me, however, was that Templeton seemed to be the ultimate badass. In Mahopac, we all went to Carmelo's Barbershop on Route 6, where the stooped-over Italian specialized in $7 bowl cuts and crew cuts. Yet here was Templeton, staring up from the magazine and newspaper pages, sporting an afro the size of Jupiter and thick wristbands midway up his arms. Even better was his attitude.

At the midway point of the 1979 season, Templeton was clearly the game's top shortstop, boasting a .317 average with 122 hits, 54 runs, and 14 stolen bases. Yet when it came to deciding a starting lineup for the All-Star Game, fans voted for Philadelphia's Larry Bowa, a far inferior player. Instead of hiding his feelings, Templeton came up with one of the sport's most enduring statements of defiance. "If I ain't startin'," he told the media, "I ain't departin'." And he didn't—the Midsummer Classic was played at Seattle's Kingdome without him.

Two years later, in the first inning of a Giants-Cardinals game at Busch Stadium, Templeton was batting when a third strike rolled past San Francisco catcher Milt May. Instead of dashing toward first, however, Templeton trotted lazily down the line before turning toward the dugout. When the crowd of 7,766 booed lustily, Templeton flashed the middle finger toward the stands. He was issued a warning by Bruce Froemming, the home-plate umpire, but in the third inning he reacted to further razzing by again flipping the bird toward St. Louis loyalists. Froemming immediately ejected Templeton from the game, and Templeton once again offered a one-finger salute. This time an enraged Herzog grabbed him by the shirt and dragged him down the dugout steps. "Get out of here!" Herzog screamed. "I don't want you on the road trip! I don't want you around my players! I don't want to see you! You make $690,000 and you go and make an ass of yourself! I don't need that and my boys don't need that!"

Had Garry Templeton really acted in such a way? I couldn't believe it. I had long been raised with certain principles and mannerisms— "Yes, Mr. Smith. No, Mr. Smith. Thank you, Mr. Smith." You never talked back and you always—*always!*—respected those around you. Especially your elders. Sure, I broke a rule or two as a kid. But never— *never!*—would I have behaved like Templeton.

Boy, oh, boy, I dug it!

From then on, Garry Templeton had a fan for life. He was the prime example that one didn't always have to go along with the crowd or take orders; that one could speak up for what he thought to be just. Although I couldn't grow an afro, I wanted to. Although I couldn't play shortstop worth a damn, I wanted to. I wanted to pivot my back foot in the batter's box the way Templeton did; wanted to wear my wristbands in the exact same spots; wanted to tell all my Little League coaches to f%#@ off. If I wasn't starting, I wasn't—uh . . . oh, wait . . . I was terrible.

On December 10, 1981, the Cardinals decided enough was enough. They sent Templeton and Sixto Lezcano to San Diego for Steve Mura and some insignificant no-hit shortstop named Ozzie Smith. I still remember first learning of the deal, thinking that "Trader" Jack McKeon, the Padres GM, had pulled off yet another steal. Templeton would move to California and put up the best numbers of his lifetime. Hell, he was only twenty-five years old. The Cardinals would never live down Templeton-for-Smith.

Never!

Ever!

Ever!

Admittedly, I should have known better. First, you can't take a tough guy like Garry Templeton, dress him up in a brown-and-yellow Taco Bell uniform, and expect him to maintain an edge. Second, by the time he arrived in San Diego, his knees were shot. He could still throw and make contact, but the onetime speed machine was a shell of his former self. He managed eight triples in 1982, then went the next four years without exceeding three. He helped the Padres reach the 1984 World Series and was selected as an All-Star reserve one season later. That, however, was about it.

In St. Louis, meanwhile, the too-good-to-be-true Smith was tearing up the league en route to a Hall of Fame career. When the dust cleared,

Templeton retired with 2,096 hits and a .271 average over sixteen seasons. Smith lasted nineteen years, accumulating 2,460 hits and a .262
average. He played in fifteen All-Star Games to Templeton's three.

That said, like all little boys unwilling to grow up, I held out hope
for Garry Templeton. With each new season I believed he would revert
to old form—or, if nothing else, at least grow back the afro and throw
ice chunks at some fans. Sadly, neither came to be. By the time Templeton retired after eighty games with the putrid New York Mets in
1991, he was a hobbled, humbled thirty-five-year-old with all the
spunk and vigor of a desert mule. I barely recognized the man, what
with his closely cropped hair and ever-widening body. It broke my
heart.

In 2000, nine years after his final major-league game, Templeton was
managing the Triple-A Edmonton Trappers of the Pacific Coast
League. Here was a riveting story, I told my editors at *Sports Illustrated*—the former bad boy now mentoring young, up-and-coming
ballplayers. It was an odd marriage, I argued, one worth exploring.
They agreed.

Upon arriving in Edmonton, I entered Templeton's small office and
was taken aback by what I saw. Though only forty-four, my hero looked
two decades older. He wore a thick mustache, his dark hair disconcert-
ingly sprinkled with salt and pepper. As we spoke, he was quiet and
low-key, sort of like a small-town librarian. He was happy to have a job
in the game, happy to be in the surroundings he most enjoyed. "His
biggest quality is his demeanor," Leon (Bull) Durham, the Trappers'
hitting coach and Templeton's onetime teammate in St. Louis, told me.
"He's not someone to get upset, no matter how bad things get. We just
lost five in a row. With some managers that's a panic. Tempy's too cool.
He teaches, not screams."

What? Was this really happening? Templeton even (gasp!) explained away his past misdeeds, saying, "I was a young, immature kid who made some mistakes." Pause. "That was a long time ago. The past is the past."

Perhaps I was in the wrong place. Perhaps this was someone else. Dickie Thon. Bobby Meacham. Craig Reynolds. Another shortstop-turned-manager. Maybe Garry Templeton had left the building, had gone elsewhere, had vanished.

Then—in a millisecond—something wonderful happened. From his pocket, the strange man sitting in front of me whipped out a pack of cigarettes and sparked up his lighter. The flame went out. He tried again, and the flame didn't take.

I looked at his face. He wasn't just annoyed. He wasn't just agitated. His expression screamed, "What the f%#@!" Someone had snuck into the kitchen and eaten the chocolate almond cake.

This was Garry Templeton.

Crash Davis

CARRIE RICKEY

I believe in the chick flick and the dick flick and that both are better when in the same movie. I believe in unprocessed bran, single-malt Scotch, and Jersey tomatoes. I believe that *Field of Dreams* and *The Natural* are such shmaltzfests they could elevate cholesterol to risky levels. I believe that the dramas of Kevin Costner are self-indulgent dreck. I believe in Title IX, ninth-inning hustle, and that catcher Crash Davis, although fictional, is as motivational a figure as Lou Gehrig.

Of course, when I invoke baseball's Iron Horse I am really comparing Costner, Crash's charismatic screen interpreter, to Gary Cooper, who essayed Gehrig in *The Pride of the Yankees*. On-screen, they are unassuming guys, consummate professionals, men who demonstrate that work ethic equals play ethic. They are ballplayers who come to the field and feel lucky for the opportunity to do what they love. They play not for the awards or the monetary rewards but, as the title of another Costner flick has it, for the love of the game.

Naturally, it's the contrasts between the movie slugger heroes that I find more telling. When Gehrig, ravaged by ALS, gave his "luckiest man on earth" farewell at Yankee Stadium, he thanked the crowd with the celebrated lines, "I have been in ballparks for seventeen years, and

159

I've never received anything but kindness and encouragement from you fans." With a nod to his fellow players—who included Joe DiMaggio, Frank Crosetti, and Lefty Gomez—he asked the assembled, "Which of you wouldn't consider it the highlight of his career just to associate with them for even one day?"

Whenever I watch *Bull Durham*—and I watch it often—I see Crash Davis as Gehrig's minor-league kindred spirit. A veteran catcher, Crash has signaled, soldiered, and dinged through twelve years in the minors and never received anything like kindness or encouragement from unruly fans or arbitrary managers. Some of his fellow players would be a trial to associate with for even a minute, let alone an entire season. Case in point: Nuke LaLoosh (Tim Robbins as a loose-jointed goofball), the rookie pitcher with a $1 million arm and 5¢ brain that suggests his slow-wittedness is in inverse velocity to his fastball.

Still, Crash shows up ready to play. He parks his ego in the locker room, recognizing that his job this season is to season Nuke, that raw side of meat, and prepare the kid for The Show. An unapologetically minor-league talent, Crash has a major-league heart. (And intellect, too. Max Patkin, the "Clown Prince of Baseball," who plays himself in the movie, says approvingly, "I saw him read a book without pictures once.")

Celebrate Gehrig's stamina and record-setting performance. Mourn his untimely death. But when you factor Crash's achievements, recognize his greater degree of difficulty. Crash has no one rooting for him. When he says good-bye to the game—and in the process breaks the minors' home-run record—the crowd could care less. His accomplishment doesn't merit so much as a brief in the *Sporting News*.

As most everyone knows, Crash Davis is the namesake of Lawrence "Crash" Davis, Durham Bulls stalwart of the 1940s. But the character, played by an appealingly irreverent Costner, is a composite of the unsung players screenwriter/director/onetime Orioles prospect Ron Shelton consorted and cavorted with in the minors during the late 1960s and early '70s. ("Don't think" is Crash's advice to Nuke on the mound and to himself at the plate. It seems also to have been Shelton's direction to Costner, who gives a refreshingly unmannered and manly performance—and who is one of the few movie stars with a major-league swing.)

Crash is decidedly *not* the heroic fantasy of the fan in the bleachers. He may well be the only movie ballplayer seen from the perspective of an actual player on the field. Which is why he's relatable in ways that slugger figures like Robert Redford's Roy Hobbs, the haloed hero of *The Natural*, never can be.

Here is the essential difference between *The Natural* and *Bull Durham*. In the climactic moment of the former, Hobbs shoots a pregnant look at the batboy, accepts "Wonderboy," his Excalibur-like stick, and proceeds to swat the ball not just out of the park but to the stars. In the anticlimactic moment of *Bull Durham*, a batboy derails Crash's train of thought by earnestly wishing him a hit. "Shut up," Crash snaps, and proceeds to strike out.

As with baseball, a movie involves us when it mirrors our own personal scenario or invites us to project our own personal drama onto it. *Bull Durham* takes me back to my primal baseball experience. That would be the summer of '63, a Dodgers/Cardinals game at Chávez Ravine. As with so many ten-year-olds before and since, once at the stadium the cheese- and chili- and chocolate-slathered food forbidden in our health-conscious household held far more fascination for me than the game. Besides, so much was going on down there in the diamond. No close-ups to clarify the action, like in a movie.

Fortunately, my dad framed the game for me as a psychological drama: "Watch how Johnny Roseboro signals to Sandy Koufax," he told me as Cardinals outfielder Curt Flood stepped up to the plate. "A lot of the game is in how the catcher and pitcher conspire to outwit the opposing batter." Dad's prompt helped me see and understand the game as something tastier than peanuts and Cracker Jacks. Thanks, *Papacito*—and *gracias*, too, to Vin Scully, that most lyrical of baseball exegetes—for sparing me the fate of the stats slut, the kind of fan more preoccupied with the numbers a ballplayer (or a movie) racks up than in what happens on the field (or on the screen).

Of all the baseball movies I've seen (and honey, I've seen 'em all, from the sunshine of *Take Me Out to the Ball Game* to the rain delay of *Mr. 3,000* to the rainout *Fear Strikes Out*), *Bull Durham* is one of the few to capture fully that catcher/pitcher conspiracy. *Bang the Drum Slowly* and *A League of Their Own* are others, but they're not so much about what happens on the field as about what happens in the heart. *Bull Durham* is about what happens in both places—and why both places matter.

Furthermore, I'm reasonably sure it's the only movie to suggest that baseball has a High Priestess. (That would be Susan Sarandon's Annie Savoy, a spiritual commissioner and carnal umpire.) Further-*most*, it's the only baseball movie that ever made me rethink the game.

Before *Bull Durham*, baseball as I understood it in all my youthful (K)oufax worship was the strikeout as the pitcher's primary objective and the no-hitter as his Holy Grail. Crash's admonition to Nuke— "Strikeouts are boring! Besides, they're fascist. Throw some ground balls, it's more democratic"—was a revelation.

Now, it would have been obvious to any guy who played Little League that a pitch resulting in a grounder upped the chances of an out or double play and had the collateral benefit of bringing glory to someone other than the hurler. But I grew up before girls played Little League. When I mentioned my "revelation" to dad, he said that if this hadn't been patently obvious to me when I was ten then he had been negligent in my baseball education.

Excluding *A League of Their Own* and *The Bad News Bears,* women in baseball movies tend to be adoring wives or that succubus Lola of *Damn Yankees.* Thus Annie Savoy is *Bull Durham*'s second revelation. Here is a woman who knows as much about the game as Crash. Here is a woman for whom baseball is a religion, who sees the ballplayer who loves the game more than it does in return, and who loves him in a way that finally puts Crash's life into balance. And he's evolved enough not to be intimidated by her.

Crash, Annie, and Nuke are a trinity: the father, mother, and unholy son of baseball. Crash and Annie are the parents who teach Nuke, that promising but wild rookie, control and consistency, and who ultimately vault him to the majors. (Despite Sarandon's and Costner's explosive on-screen chemistry, off-screen it was she and Robbins who hooked up, going the distance for twenty-three years and two children. Was it those sessions on consistency?) While Annie's tutorials help Nuke respect the game's mystique, Crash's example helps him respect the game.

So when Nuke shakes off his signals, Crash alerts the batter what the knucklehead-without-a-knuckleball is about to throw. Even on the receiving end of a fight, Crash can extract a life lesson for his pupil/assailant. Floored by Nuke's fist, Crash has the presence of mind to immediately demand, "Didja hit me with your right hand or didja hit me with your left?" Informed it was Nuke's glove side, Crash says, "That's good. When you get in a fight with a drunk, don't hit 'im with your pitching hand."

From hygiene to humility, Crash is a deep well of wisdom, and as a dispenser of sage advice he ranks up there with Vito Corleone.

"You'll never make it to the bigs with fungus on your shower shoes," Crash instructs Nuke. "Think classy, you'll be classy. If you win twenty in The Show, you can let the fungus grow back and the press will think you're colorful."

Crash's sermon on how to handle sportswriters is an evergreen. His pupil's ego so inflated that it couldn't fit in a stadium, let alone a locker room, he right-sizes it by introducing Nuke to the homilies of humbleness and helpfulness. "Learn your clichés," Crash says, aware that inside these moldering chestnuts are kernels of truth about the game. "Study them. Know them. They're your friends."

- *We gotta play 'em one day at a time.*
- *I'm just happy to be here and hope I can help the club.*
- *I just wanta give it my best shot, and Good Lord willing, things'll work out.*

Chief among Crash's many admirable traits is the switch-hitter's ability to digest, process, and adjust. When first we meet him, he strolls into the Bulls' front office introducing himself as "the player to be named later." Advised that his job is to polish Nuke, that diamond in the rough, Crash rounds the bases of grief in about a minute, entirely skipping bargaining and depression. Denial: "My Triple-A contract gets bought out so I can hold some flavor-of-the-month's dick in the bus leagues?" Anger: "I quit! I fuckin' quit!" Acceptance: "Who we play tomorrow?"

Here is a guy who knows, in the words of everyone's high school coach, that there is no "I" in "team." For this, and for so many other reasons, isn't it time Crash got some love from Cooperstown?

Greg Maddux
NEAL POLLACK

I got to witness many great feats of the steroid era. When Mark McGwire and Sammy Sosa were chasing seventy, I had a good view from my usual midprice seat at Wrigley. I was there at Chávez Ravine the night Eric Gagné started his consecutive save streak, and the night it ended. The arrival of Manny Ramirez to L.A. filled my heart with joy and wonder and gave me hope for a brighter tomorrow. And even though I, like every other human being outside the Bay Area, find Barry Bonds to be a totally loathsome near-monster, I still made sure to be at Dodger Stadium to boo him on as he approached Aaron's record.

But nothing as a baseball fan has ever given me more pleasure than watching Greg Maddux pitch. It was like being in the presence of a great sculptor or tai chi master. On his best nights, he controlled the game more thoroughly than any player of his time. He didn't waste a single pitch, and never hitch-stepped off the mound when a bunt came his way. Maddux wasn't a lob-to-first to keep the runner "honest" type of pitcher. He knew where every runner was, at every moment, and he knew exactly what he needed to do to optimize his chances of getting them. He played like this for a very long time.

I saw him during his raw years with the Cubs—until he won his first Cy Young, in 1992—and during his glory years, when Atlanta came to town. The worst (but still above-average) part of his career, the late-years return to Chicago, passed me by (save his occupying a permanent roster spot on my fantasy team). But when the Dodgers traded Cesar Izturis to the Cubs and got back an aged, fading Maddux in return, it was the most excited I'd been as a fan in years. Now, at last, I could root for my favorite team and my favorite player at the same time. Propped up by the excitement of a pennant race, and probably enjoying the warm weather given his now-aching bones, he didn't disappoint.

This wasn't the Maddux of the '90s. Most of the time, he could only go six. One start out of three, the opposing hitters figured him out the second time through the order—he'd get lit up for five runs capped by a three-run homer and would have to come out in the fourth inning. But other times he'd return to total dominance, like an old dog briefly remembering his puppyhood during a surprise open sprint across the park. Those games were the best.

One Sunday afternoon in August 2006, I went to Dodger Stadium to watch him pitch against the Giants during the heat of an awesome pennant race. It was vintage Maddux. There were no dramatic confrontations that blew Bonds out of his shoes. No balls got thrown to the fence. It was just little pop-ups and groundouts. Occasionally, someone would get a single, but the next batter would inevitably hit into a double play. Then there'd be a weak grounder to third, and it was time to watch Diamond Vision for a couple of minutes.

I didn't watch the score that night, because no one on either team could score. In the visitors' dugout sat Jason Schmidt, a good pitcher having a really good night. He went eight innings, struck out nine, walked one, and gave up five hits, all of them singles save a double to Russell Martin. But the real stats story happened down the right-field line, where someone digitally kept track of Maddux's pitch count. His pitches simply didn't add at a normal pace. As the innings went by, his pitch-per-inning average actually went down. A six-pitch inning followed an eight-pitch inning. I believe he even had a *five*-pitch inning. He walked off the mound after eight innings having given up no runs, two hits, and no walks. Four batters struck out. He did it all in 68 pitches. It took Schmidt 115 pitches to do essentially the same thing. Guess which pitcher had career-ending shoulder surgery the following season.

I'd seen guys throw sixty-eight pitches in two innings. This guy threw them in eight, and he was forty years old. Oh, yes, the Dodgers won the game 1–0 in ten innings, when Martin hit a walk-off homer off Vinny Chulk. That was pretty cool, too, but not as cool as what the game's real star had done. I'd seen Toulouse-Lautrec at the Moulin Rouge, visited Gauguin in Haiti, and sat in while Picasso dreamed up cubism. Or maybe I'd just seen Greg Maddux pitch. But art is art, no matter what form it takes.

In an era when his contemporaries were bulking up like Popeye in the chase for glory and five-year, $47 million contracts, Maddux sat in the dugout, glasses on, and studied. He was the pitcher as permanent graduate student, always taking notes, making observations, and thinking. For the bookish division of the baseball fan base, he made a perfect role model. Even though he was an exceptionally talented athlete, compared with the mega-sluggers and their bulging neck muscles, he seemed like one of us. I appreciated it, because baseball nerds have no credibility. "One of us," to a baseball fan, usually means a talentless lunch-bucket hustler like Ryan Freel or a fat, John Kruk–style homer guy. Rarely do players directly cater to the scorekeeping brain.

While half of baseball 'roided out during Maddux's career, the game also underwent its most profound philosophical shift since racial integration. As Brady Anderson hit his shady fifty-two, the stat dorks rattled the gates, waving their *Baseball Abstracts* and crying WHIP. Statistics told the real story of the game; some stats told it more accurately than others, and no stats (other than, maybe, Ichiro's) told it better than Greg Maddux's. He pitched like a calculator.

For a while, I played an online simulation game where I drafted teams from a pool made up of every season for every player who's ever put on a major-league uniform, going back to the 1880s. There was a salary cap, so unless I wanted a pitching staff with a collective ERA over 7.0, I couldn't have Ted Williams and Babe Ruth in the same lineup. There'd be no money left for anyone else. Of all the available seasons, of every available player, very few were more valuable than 1995 Greg Maddux. He sat high in the pantheon, above 1968 Bob Gibson and 1965 Sandy Koufax, on equal footing with the best of Christy Mathewson. Only Cy Young was above, and then only because he pitched 500 innings before breakfast.

Maddux's 1995 numbers, in an age of records artificially broken, may never be seen again. He pitched 209.2 innings that year. From there, I must italicize his feats. He won nineteen games and lost *two*, with an earned average of *1.63*. He gave up 147 hits, only 8 home runs, and walked 23 batters while striking out 181. His WHIP, or ratio of base runners per innings pitched, came to an astonishing *0.811*. In other words, on his way to his sixth of seventeen Gold Gloves and his fourth consecutive Cy Young Award, Maddux allowed fewer than one base runner per inning.

Let's keep going. In those two losses, his worst games of the year, he gave up five earned runs to both the Rockies and Reds. Meanwhile, he gave up five earned runs in the *entire month of June*, seven in July, and *one* in September. With Maddux on the mound that year, the Braves were almost guaranteed a victory. That was also the year he got his only World Series title. In the year of their seventy-home-run chase,

McGwire and Sosa didn't win diddly, but Maddux's finest hour scored him a ring.

In a time of heat and power, he exuded coolness and control. He led the league in games started seven times, the final time in 2005, when he was thirty-nine years old. In that season, he walked thirty-six guys in 225 innings. In 1996, he pitched 245 innings and walked twenty-eight. In a career where Maddux pitched 5,008 innings, he walked only 999 batters. That's a recipe for winning 355 games. I'm grateful that I got to witness some of them.

In 2008, after management had inexplicably let him go to the Padres for a season and a half, he came back to the Dodgers for a short curtain call. He made some great starts—a seven-inning 1–0 loss in Colorado, the most hitter-friendly park in the history of baseball—and some bad ones, like when the Phillies touched him for nine hits and two mammoth homers. That was understandable; the Phillies were on their way to the World Series. But the Padres and Nationals also roughed him up. Clearly, the end was nigh.

I made sure to get to his last start at Dodger Stadium, the second-to-last start of his career. It was a sad and dispiriting affair against the Giants, who got him on the mat with a two-run single in the first and never let him get up. A two-run homer by Bengie Molina capped a four-run fifth, and his night ended there, in a 7–1 loss, outdueled by Barry Zito and his sixteen losses. For once, Maddux, who for twenty years had come to the ballpark looking as crisp as a freshly pressed potato chip, appeared old, sagged, and even a little jowly.

But redemption came a few days later, in San Francisco. He gave up two hits and no walks, with the only run coming on Randy Winn's solo homer in the fourth. In six innings, he threw forty-seven pitches, thirty-eight of them for strikes. Even at the end, Maddux controlled a baseball as though it were a yo-yo attached to his hand by a ninety-foot string.

As I watched that game on TV, clicking off pitches in my head like an autistic computer programmed to do only one thing, I felt almost incomparably sad, which isn't usual for me when the Dodgers are winning. Maddux, only four years older than me, had been playing professional baseball for my entire adult lifetime. I was a college student when he started, and in the month before his retirement, I was a father pushing forty. Our lives didn't exactly run parallel—I wasn't a multi-mega-millionaire and hadn't been at the top of my profession for most of the past two decades—but I still considered his career my own.

When you're a kid, your idols are aspirational figures, and when you're old, they're objects of nostalgia. But when you're in your prime, you choose your heroes as proxy. As a child, my favorite player was Steve Garvey, later revealed as a cheap, philandering douche. Now it's a guy named Matt Kemp, an exciting five-tooler but hardly an awesome intellect. In my twenties and thirties, though, I went for the players who seemed smart, who played their game like it was a science. In basketball, that was Steve Nash, and in baseball, it was Greg Maddux. I could never accomplish what he did, but I could understand and appreciate the way he went about his business. Given the unlikely opportunity, it's how I would have wanted to play ball myself.

Please indulge one more game description before we leave the Mad Dog memory machine. It was August 3, 2006, in Cincinnati, during Maddux's first stint with the Dodgers. After five innings, when he walked off the mound, the Dodgers' announcer said, "We might have something special brewing here." Maddux hadn't given up a hit. He pitched a hitless sixth, too. And then it started to rain.

There'd already been a delay before the start of the game, and this one lasted almost two hours. When play resumed, even though he had a two-run lead and a no-hitter in progress, Maddux didn't go out for the seventh. In the least dramatic such moment in baseball history, Scott Hatteberg hit a single off Joe Beimel, and the no-hitter died.

Maybe it would have continued if he had gone back out, or maybe his arm would have fallen off. Regardless, you know it was his decision, and looking at the numbers, I can understand his logic. Though he gave up no hits, he had walked three batters. He'd thrown seventy-two pitches in six innings, only forty-one for strikes.

Clearly, he didn't have his best stuff.

| _Bobby Murcer_ | | ◇ | ◇ | ◇ | |
| STEFAN FATSIS | | | | | |

1. Bobby Murcer Gave Me Gum

I think it was Dubble Bubble. From a big white tub on a ledge against the rear wall of the home locker room in Yankee Stadium. August 24, 1972. He told me to help myself. I took a single piece and held it in my hand, unsure whether to chew now or save for later. "Thanks, Bobby," I might have muttered. Or "Thanks, Mr. Murcer." Or just "Thanks." I don't recall a conversation, whether he asked me how old I was (nine) or what position I played (shortstop) or who my favorite player was (him). Maybe he mussed my bowl cut and said, inspirationally, that if I fielded lots of grounders I could make it to the big leagues someday. In the Zapruder film of our lives, that's what star athletes do to awestruck little kids, isn't it?

My first visit to a professional clubhouse came courtesy of a family friend who leveraged a part-time gig hosting an interview show on a 500-watt radio station in Westchester County to score press credentials at New York stadiums. Over the years, he befriended the Yankees' security guys. So when he, his son, Steve, and I arrived before the

Mayor's Trophy Game—a midseason Yankees-Mets charity exhibition—we were waved in. As vividly as my moment in the athletes' sanctum, I recall the family friend asking my mother's permission to take me there. He worried that I might see the players "in their BVDs."

There's no dramatic twist here. Bobby Murcer wasn't a jerk. He didn't refuse me an autograph. (I didn't ask for one.) He didn't drop an F-bomb, or his drawers. Nothing happened in that brief encounter that would sour me on him or any other athlete. I shook his hand, and we moved on to the next Yankee—Horace Clarke? Roy White? Future first designated hitter Ron Blomberg? Future wife swapper Fritz Peterson?—and then down the tunnel to the dugout and onto the field, where Steve and I were photographed with Sparky Lyle, who would lead the American League that season with thirty-five saves. That's me on the left, hands on the hips of my blue-and-red tie-dyed pants, squinting into the lens, the amply sideburned Lyle resting his Wilson on my right shoulder. The picture was published in our local newspaper.

Did I wish I had posed with Bobby? Disappointment wasn't possible that day. In the game, he went 0 for 2 before being replaced by Johnny Callison. But I'd met him. That and the gum were enough.

2. Bobby Murcer Batted .331; I Batted .750

What attracts a fan to a player? Talent, position, statistics, appearance—the quantity *x* itself, to quote Salinger. But the most powerful connection is forged in the imagination. In mine, Bobby Murcer and I were on parallel baseball paths. He was signed in 1964 as an eighteen-year-old next Mickey Mantle—from Oklahoma (just like the Mick), wooed by scout Tom Greenwade (just like the Mick), a shortstop who needed to move to the outfield (just like the Mick)—and then spent the better part of three years in the minors and two more in the army.

I was born in 1963 and did my own apprenticeship in the bush leagues—diapers, nursery school, kindergarten. In 1969, Bobby entered the starting lineup and I entered grade school. In 1970, he became the full-time center fielder and I became a full-time fan of a Yankees team that finished in second place in the American League East. Our futures were bright.

We both had breakout seasons in 1971. Bobby batted .331, stroked twenty-five homers, drove in ninety-four runs, and led the league in on-base percentage and on-base plus slugging (not that anyone was measuring OB and OPS then). I debuted as a shortstop and pitcher—mercifully, tee ball had not yet arrived in my town—for the purple-shirted Bisons of the Pelham Little League. In 1972, Bobby hit thirty-three homers, drove in ninety-six runs, and scored a league-leading 102 runs. Back on the Bisons, I batted .750 (aided, no doubt, by some generous self-scoring), with eighteen hits in twenty-four at bats, including a grand slam that raced through the left side of the infield and past the chasing outfielders; I can still see the ball rolling, feel myself rounding second, hear the parents and players cheering. I was the best player on my team, a Little League star. Bobby was the best player on his team, too, an A.L. All-Star. We had so much in common.

It's only in retrospect, examining Bobby's stats and my own (I saved them), that the parallel arcs of our baseball careers truly become clear. He peaked at age twenty-six. I peaked at nine. We were both solid for one more season—Bobby going .304, twenty-two, and ninety-five in 1973; me pitching, anchoring the infield, and batting .500 for the next-level-up Cherokees. And that was pretty much it. Bobby hit just ten home runs in 1974, which he forever blamed on playing in cavernous Shea Stadium while the real stadium—the uppercase Stadium—underwent renovation. The Yankees traded him, breaking my heart, to San Francisco that winter (for Bobby Bonds). He hit eleven homers in 1975, twenty-three in '76, and was shipped to the Chicago Cubs (for Bill

Madlock), where he had a respectable '77 (.265, twenty-seven, eighty-nine) and a lousy '78 (.281, nine, sixty-four). I, meanwhile, moved up to real Little League, the eleven- and twelve-year-old version that culminates with the World Series in Williamsport, Pennsylvania. I played sparingly during my first season on the Jets, a star no more, and when I did it was at second base. The next season, I led off and batted a respectable .363 with sixteen hits—fifteen of them singles.

My own baseball reality was clear: I was no longer the best player on the field, and by far the smallest. When, in 1976 and in seventh grade, I moved up to the Senior League—sixty feet six inches from the mound to home, ninety feet between the bases—I didn't stand a chance. In 1978, my final year of organized ball, I started almost every game but batted a pathetic .175—four hits in twenty-three at bats. (Once I was thrown out at first base by the center fielder playing on the edge of the outfield grass.) Bobby's reality also was clear. He wasn't the next Mantle—not that he ever expected to be—just a serviceable starting outfielder with power that ebbed too early. We both fell short of our early promise. We had that in common, too.

3. Bobby Murcer Was a Yankee in 1971

By all logic, I should have dropped Bobby along with my Hot Wheels collection and Panasonic Toot-a-Loop Radio when the Yankees finally became good and then great. I attended World Series games in the Bronx in 1976, '77, and '78, and dozens of regular-season ones, hopping the No. 5 train at Dyer Avenue, changing to the 4 at Grand Concourse, and navigating the crowds to my friend's father's corporate box seats behind the first-base dugout. But if I had to choose a team to represent my life, a team that would follow me like a Greek chorus, a team that I could point to and say, "Understand this and you will better understand me," it would be the '71 Yankees.

They were the apotheosis of mediocrity, the ideal representative of the CBS-owned generation of lousy clubs between the Ruth-Gehrig-DiMaggio-Mantle dynasties of 1927–1964 and the Steinbrenner-free agency-new stadium powerhouses of 1976–1981. Not a Hall of Famer among them. Barely an *All-Star* among them. But I admired, and still do, their superstarlessness; even as an eight-year-old Little League prospect, I somehow understood that being just good enough—being Bobby—was a safe aspiration. Rooting for the Yankees then didn't imply arrogance or entitlement. It implied humility, a tolerance for disappointment, and a love of the obscure. I was cool with that.

There was the dignified, pigeon-toed Roy White in left. The oldest Alou brother, Felipe, in right. Big John Ellis and "See Ya Later" Danny Cater at first. At second, "Hoss" Clarke, with a stance that spanned the batter's box from back to front. At short, the "slick-fielding" (i.e., "weak-hitting") future general manager Gene "The Stick" Michael. At third, Jerry Kenney, who batted .193 in 1970 and still kept his job. A young Thurman Munson catching, backed up by Jake Gibbs, whose signature adorned my Bat Day bat. The starting pitchers: Mel Stottlemyre, Stan Bahnsen, Steve Kline, and Peterson and his fellow future wife swapper Mike Kekich. Out of the bullpen, the high-kicking Lindy McDaniel.

And, in center, Bobby. He earned a two-page color profile in the '71 Yankees Yearbook—only the stars got color double-truck treatment—that, in the tradition of sports media guides, fashion magazines, and communist dictatorships, airbrushed any flaws. Sure, Bobby batted just .257 in '70. But he hit four consecutive home runs during a doubleheader! He had a stretch of thirty-one hits in seventy-nine at bats in June! He tied the league best with fifteen outfield assists! "At 24," read the copy (probably written by Bob Fishel, the Yankees P.R. man, who years earlier had signed the midget Eddie Gaedel to play for Bill Veeck in St. Louis), "Murcer is a young Yankee whose bat, arm, legs, and desire will make the Yankees champions again." God, I hoped so.

But I was happy to have him no matter his stats or the team's final record, which was 82–80.

4. Bobby Murcer Wore No. 1

So I wore No. 1. I might have worn it anyway, because I was the smallest kid on the field and No. 1 always adorned the smallest jersey. Plus, I was a prototypically scrappy little guy, and proto-scrappers are obligated to wear No. 1—I believe it's in the Little League rulebook. But it was really out of Bobby worship.

I looked and played nothing like he did. I was a singles-hitting middle infielder who batted right. Bobby batted left, played the outfield, and hit home runs—or did, anyway, when I became a sentient fan (and we remember athletes in their greatness, not their decline, or at least we're most attentive to them in their greatness).

Independently, the number made sense for both of us. No. 1 turned Bobby's body into an unbroken line. During the long, looping practice swings I mimicked during playground stickball and backyard Wiffle ball—whatever modest switch-hitting ability I possess I owe to Bobby—his body swayed diaphanously toward the pitcher and back. His uniform number enhanced the image: Bobby as metronome. And the actual swing—man, could Bobby Murcer roll his wrists and extend his forearms. Straight lines everywhere. No. 1.

When Bobby eventually returned to the Yankees—heartbreakingly missing the championships—the team was managed by Billy Martin, who had reclaimed the No. 1 he wore in the 1950s. (Bobby Richardson had it between Martin and Murcer.) So Bobby took No. 2. I was done with baseball by then, but in soccer I reflexively chose No. 2.

And when the Yankees retired No. 1 in 1986? I like to think it was for Bobby, not Billy.

5. Bobby Murcer Hit Two Home Runs in One Game

I saw Bobby play in person at least eleven times—ten in the old, original stadium; one in the renovated version. I say "at least" because I can verify only those from the collection of ticket stubs I keep stuffed in a cigar box. (Bering Corona Grande, my father's preferred smoke, 35¢ apiece. They stank.) There were certainly more games—there isn't a stub extant from 1973 or '74; or from the Gibbs Bat Day; or from my first visit in '69, a doubleheader attended with my older brother. (I would have been six, he fourteen. I have no idea who accompanied us, certainly not my Greek immigrant father, who didn't understand the game or my ardor. We sat in the mezzanine behind home plate. I ate too much ice cream and was obsessed with the pigeons roosting in the rafters.)

It would make sense that Bobby did something in one of those confirmed early visits to earn my affection. Apparently not, according to retrosheet.org, the fact-checking, truth-telling, memory-enhancing repository of major-league box scores and play-by-play accounts. July 19, 1970: Bobby goes 0 for 7 in a Sunday afternoon doubleheader sweep at the hands of the California Angels witnessed by me and 52,324 other customers paying $1, $1.50, $2.75, or $4. August 9, 1970: a doubleheader split with Baltimore. Bobby is one for four in the opener and one for five in the second game. June 27, 1971: another twinbill. Bobby goes 0 for 4 and two for three—meaningless singles both—in a sweep by the lowly Washington Senators.

On September 18, 1971, Bobby finally delivers: two doubles, a triple, two runs scored, and four RBIs in a 9–0 rout of Cleveland that requires just two hours and eight minutes. July 21, 1972: In the first game of yet another doubleheader, Bobby—batting third behind Clarke and Munson—homers twice, off of California's Lloyd Allen. Peterson pitches a complete game, and the Yanks win 6–0 in two hours and sixteen minutes. In the nightcap, Bobby bats fifth, singles, and scores a run in a 3–0 complete-game victory for Stottlemyre. Time of game: one hour, fifty-six minutes.

I could have watched baseball eight hours a day then, but still, two-hour games—two-hour *day* games—sure made it easy to be a young fan. So did witnessing your idol belt two homers into the green outfield seats of Yankee Stadium. I wish I could remember exactly what that felt like. Thrilling. Joyful. Very, very personal. Surely he hit them for me.

6. Bobby Murcer Drove in Five Runs in One Game

In 1970, ex-Yankee Jim Bouton's baseball diary *Ball Four* was published. The book definitively and hilariously demythologized professional athletes in general and the Yankees in particular. (It also helpfully added the terms "shitfuck," "fuckshit," and "beaver shooting" to the linguistic corpus.) But I didn't read *Ball Four* until my midteens. In the wider sports media of the day there remained little from which a kid, or a parent, could glean a player's true personality. A canned quote, a pregame interview, a chance autograph signing—goodness and badness just weren't readily detectable. Even if behind the locker-room or bedroom door your favorite player was, in fact, a complete jerk, chances were you'd never find out. There were no drug tests or *SportsCenter*s or Deadspins to expose him as a fraud or even, more simply, as routinely, mundanely, humanly flawed. If hero worship isn't dead, it's on its deathbed, and maybe it should be.

So when I chose Bobby, I had no idea whether he was a sinner or saint. That he turned out to be the latter—in his anodyne autobiography, the only vice to which he confessed was chewing tobacco and, for a short time, shilling for that industry (no word on whether, like many players in the '60s and '70s, he partook of the occasional amphetamine, or "greenie")—was a bonus realized only in time, specifically after June 26, 1979, when Bobby returned from his New York exile in a trade with Chicago for a minor-league pitcher. He was no longer the second coming of Mantle, just a thirty-three-year-old corner outfielder with a fat salary ($320,000) and a thinning bat who'd been granted a final baseball wish: to end his career where it began.

The Yankees trailed the Orioles by ten games, and it was obvious there would be no third consecutive championship. Amid the usual chaos that defined the era, Steinbrenner had rehired Martin for a second tour as manager (of an eventual five). Reggie Jackson was hurt. Closer Goose Gossage had torn a ligament in his thumb while punching teammate Cliff Johnson in a fight in the locker-room showers. And then, on August 2, an off day for the team, Munson was killed when the small jet he was piloting crashed at an airport in Canton, Ohio, where he lived.

Bobby and outfielder Lou Piniella were Munson's closest friends on the team, and they spoke at the funeral four days later. Piniella read from Ecclesiastes. Bobby began his eulogy before more than five hundred people in the Canton Civic Center by reading from a poem by a New York writer and educator named Angelo Patri: "The life of a soul on earth lasts longer than his departure. . . . He lives on in your life and the lives of all others who knew him." Sobbing, Bobby continued in his own words: "He lived. He led. He loved."

I was visiting relatives in suburban Detroit when the news broke. Like countless other fans, I wept. On the day after Munson's death, the Yankees played, as scheduled, losing to Baltimore 1–0 in the opener of a four-game series at home. They lost the second game and won the third. Bobby and Piniella and their wives flew to Canton immediately afterward to be with Munson's widow, Diana, before the funeral the next day. The rest of the Yankees followed on an early-morning charter. As soon as the ceremony ended, the team flew back to New York for the finale against the Orioles, which was ABC's *Monday Night Baseball* game of the week. Keith Jackson did the play-by-play. Howard Cosell and Don Drysdale handled the color. I watched the game at my aunt and uncle's house, alternating innings between couch and floor.

Ron Guidry started for New York. He had a 9–7 record at the time—a far cry from his Cy Young Award–winning 25–3 the previous, magical season. (Guidry would, however, win nine of his last ten decisions.) Through six innings, Baltimore led 4–0. How the Yankees were managing to play at all astonished me even then. But Thurman would have wanted it, they said, and that was understandably admirable, like something out of an old sports movie, *Knute Rockne: All American* or *Brian's Song*. The great ones play through their tears.

Except for pinch-running in the ninth inning of one game, Bobby hadn't played in the series. But he told Martin he wanted to be in the lineup that night. He played left field and batted second. For Cosell, his appearance signified great drama ahead. Not only had Bobby just stepped off a plane after burying his teammate, he hadn't done much since rejoining the Yankees—in thirty games, a .220 batting average, no homers, and just five runs batted in. "He might break out," Cosell intoned when Bobby came to the plate in the third inning, "at any time." In his first three at bats, he struck out, flied out, and lined out.

Through six and two-thirds innings, Orioles starter Dennis Martinez had allowed just three hits. Then Bucky Dent walked and Willie Randolph doubled to left field, sending Dent to third. Up came Bobby.

The crowd of 36,314 stood.

I edged closer to the television.

And Bobby hit the ball out, over the right-field fence.

He was supposed to have cleared that wall so many more times than he had—it was his 141st homer as a Yankee—but that didn't matter now: Bobby had homered for Thurman. Bobby had laid to rest his best friend; donned a pinstriped uniform with a sad, black armband; and homered for him. "You could see," Cosell said in his typical staccato bombast, "he was ready to erupt."

But in the bottom of the ninth the Yankees were still losing 4–3. Tippy Martinez replaced Dennis Martinez. Dent led off with another walk. Martinez threw Randolph's bunt past first, and both runners advanced a base. Up stepped Bobby. He fell behind in the count, no balls and two strikes. And then he lashed a single into left field. Dent scored. Randolph followed. The Yankees won, 5–4.

7. Bobby Murcer Died

If I had to pick the moment when my childhood ended, that no-out single would be as good as any. I was sixteen. My father had died, of a brain tumor, three months earlier. And my fanhood was, if not ebbing, then at least changing. In the space of three years, my team had given me more lifetime sports memories than a kid deserved: Chris Chambliss's pennant-winning walk-off homer against Kansas City in '76 (from the postgame rampage my oldest brother brought back a hunk of sod, which I saved in a plastic sandwich bag until the grass turned brown); Jackson's three dingers in Game Six in '77 (it's painful to admit, but I missed the last two because the family friend who brought me wanted to leave to beat the traffic); and, perhaps best of all, the comeback from fourteen games down to the Red Sox and Dent's three-run homer in the one-game playoff in '78 (which I listened to on a transistor radio during JV soccer practice). There also was the time I launched a paper airplane from the left-field upper deck that hit Jim Rice in the ass; he calmly bent over, picked it up, and stuffed it in his back pocket.

And then grieving Bobby's nationally televised five RBIs that August night. The narrative of my childhood was complete.

For the next three seasons, Bobby hung around on the Yankees' bench. He didn't play much, and he didn't do much when he did. In the first three months of the 1983 season, Bobby played in just nine games. One day in late June, Steinbrenner called to "ask" whether he might want to retire and join Phil Rizzuto, Frank Messer, and Bill White in the Yankees' broadcast booth. The Boss gave him thirty minutes to decide. Bobby did the mental calculus: He was thirty-seven—ancient in the preconditioning, preweightlifting, pre-PEDs early '80s. He wasn't playing. There wasn't much of a market for old pinch hitters batting under .200, and he didn't want to leave New York again anyway. When George called back, Bobby said yes. He was on the air that night.

By then I was away at college, and over the next several seasons I would catch only a handful of Yankees broadcasts. I moved overseas. I spent a year in dreaded Boston. In my midtwenties, I returned to New York and began watching—and caring—again. Bobby was part of the WPIX broadcast crew, but I sublimated the old feelings. I wasn't nine anymore, after all. It was like the line from the Dire Straits song "Romeo and Juliet." Oh, Bobby? Yeah, you know, I used to have a scene with him.

But it was more than that. I didn't want to know this Murcer (to Rizzuto he was always "Murcer," just as White was "White" and Messer "Messer"). This wasn't my idol, the guy whose rhythmic swing I needed to emulate, whose number I needed to wear. This was a folksy ex-player who had both a lot and not very much to say. He wasn't especially insightful. He wasn't especially funny. He wasn't especially anything, except an interrupter of the voices of my youth. They weren't supposed to be talking to Bobby; they were supposed to be talking *about* him, on the wooden box with the knobs and the color picture in the "TV room" with the orange wall-to-wall carpet in my suburban childhood home. Bobby was my hero, and heroes belong in a time capsule. They're not supposed to grow older.

And yet they do. On December 24, 2006, Bobby was diagnosed with a brain tumor. On July 12, 2008, he died. Current and former Yankees, and Yankees fans, remembered him as kind, considerate, nice, authentic. A gentleman. A class act. A True Yankee. He loved his teammates. He mentored young players. He told a good story. He believed in God. One fan, commenting online about Bobby's obituary in the *New York Times,* said he deserved a plaque in Monument Park beyond the fence in center field.

There were other, more prosaic but no less important measurements of Bobby's baseball life. He played seventeen seasons in the majors and broadcast for another twenty-three. He hit 252 home runs, among them his first big-league hit and his last. He played in the All-Star Game five times. He was the third Yankee, after DiMaggio and Mantle, to earn $100,000 in a season. He played on some of the worst Yankees teams ever, and just missed playing on some of the best. He was worthy of my adoration. He gave me a piece of gum.

Mookie Wilson
MICHAEL IAN BLACK

If I have any excuse at all, it is that I was eleven.

At that age, I still believed there was a very good chance that I was going to grow up to become a major-league baseball player. I played Little League, made the all-star team two years in a row, and considered myself a likely first-round draft pick by one of the New York teams. My friends, of course, thought the same thing about themselves, and while I recognized that they were utterly delusional, I did not reach the same conclusion about myself. (But that, I suppose, is the point of self-delusion. If you knew you suffered from it, you wouldn't be suffering from it.)

Because we all considered ourselves to be future major leaguers (and probably Hall of Fame candidates to boot), it was a big deal to everybody when it was announced that Mookie Wilson would be coming to speak to our local Little League. This was probably 1983, a few years before he famously hit the dribbler that squeaked through Bill Buckner's legs in Game Six of the World Series, sending the Mets to the decisive seventh game, where they won the championship.

At the time, Wilson was known primarily as an eager, dependable center fielder with a funny nickname. But I didn't really care who he was—the point was, a real major-league baseball player was coming to our town! To talk to us! About baseball! And we could get his autograph! It was unbelievable. The thought of meeting an actual professional baseball player seemed almost as far-fetched as meeting Ms. Pac-Man.

In my mind, ballplayers inhabited a different, better universe. The kind that was populated only with athletes, astronauts, assorted rock musicians, and Christie Brinkley. It was certainly a better place to live than my constrictive New Jersey town. Even at eleven, I knew I was going to leave there as soon as I could. Baseball playing seemed like a reasonable option, as did long-haul trucking.

My plan for that evening was to secure a front-row, premium seat. I would be front and center, the better to see Wilson speak, and the better for him to see me, and, perhaps, recognize that I too held the spark of baseball greatness. It was entirely possible, I secretly thought, that Mookie would ask me to stay afterward and invite me to join a super-secret baseball academy for eleven-year-old future baseball stars like myself. Yes, I would say. Yes, Mookie Wilson, I would like to attend your super-secret baseball academy.

So that's where I was. Front row, center, in the middle school auditorium waiting with a couple hundred boys and girls just like myself. Waiting to see what an actual major-league baseball player looked like in person. How tall would he be? How strong? Would he crush baseballs in his hand? What would he talk about? Honestly, I didn't care if he talked at all. All he had to do was exist in the same space as me for my evening to feel worthwhile.

A detail about the evening that strikes me as funny in retrospect is that we all wore our baseball uniforms. Maybe it was required by the Little League, I don't know, but it seems like a peculiar thing to have us do. It would be like wearing a postal uniform to go get the mail. The only person that night who wasn't wearing a baseball uniform was

Mookie Wilson, who wore a sport coat and a nice pair of pants. (Now that I am older, I also find it funny when adults wear baseball uniforms to stadiums, as if by wearing a Derek Jeter jersey, you are either increasing Jeter's chances of doing well or increasing your own chances of actually becoming Derek Jeter.)

The whole room was buzzing with that giddy excitement kids have when they know something INCREDIBLY AWESOME is about to happen. We were all bouncing in our seats, laughing, poking each other in our polyester uniform jerseys. We were acting like the idiots we were.

When Mookie finally came out, the room erupted with applause. There he was, the perfect embodiment of all of our dreams. Surprisingly, he looked like a normal guy. A normal, I must add at this point, black guy.

At the time, Hillsborough, New Jersey, was a new suburban town carved from a failing agricultural industry, and remaking itself into a New York bedroom community. I lived there from the time I was five until I left for college at seventeen. Back then the town was overwhelmingly white. Probably 85 or 90 percent. So my experience with black people was somewhat limited. I didn't have any black friends, didn't really know any black people. Nor did I think I harbored any particular prejudices against black people. My experience with African Americans was primarily limited to my two favorite TV shows, *The Cosby Show* and *What's Happening!!* I certainly didn't consider myself a racist. At eleven, I'm not sure I even knew what a racist was.

Mookie took the stage, as I said, to great applause. We were all legitimately thrilled to see him, and of course, we were still giddy from the buildup. In short, we were freaking out.

I have no idea what he said to us that night, save for two things. The first was how he got his memorable nickname. His grandmother in South Carolina gave it to him because of the funny way he pronounced the word *milk* as a toddler. My reaction to the second thing he said prompted me to write this essay, because ever since I have filed away the moment in the "Try to Forget" file in my memory.

He said, "And then when I went to college . . . "

And I laughed. Out loud.

I laughed because Mookie Wilson, a black guy with a ridiculous nickname, was talking about going to college. My immediate impulse was to laugh, and in that moment, I understood a deep and horrible truth about myself, although it was something I could not have put into words at the time.

It's this: I felt superior to Mookie Wilson, a guy who embodied everything I wanted for myself, who played for the New York Mets, who was famous and richer than I would ever be, who was talented and strong, who was loved by an entire metropolitan region. In that moment, I recognized that, despite all of that, I felt superior to Mookie Wilson for the simple reason that he was black.

You can be a complete asshole when you are eleven. I am living proof.

He heard me laugh, and our eyes met for half a second. I don't know if he understood why I was laughing or not, but there was nothing accusatory in his eyes. He just looked a little confused.

Years later, I was in New York City watching some guys hustle tourists in a game of three-card monte. One rube, an Asian guy who didn't really speak English, took out $20 to play, then decided at the last moment to withdraw his money, probably correctly sensing he could not win. The guy running the game grabbed at the guy's cash, insisting that he had committed to the game. I butted in, telling him to leave the Asian guy alone, that he didn't understand. Out of nowhere, another guy came up and punched me in the jaw. I didn't fall. Instead, I remember feeling astonished. In the half-second after the assault and before the entire three-card monte crew fled, my assailant and I locked eyes, and I'm pretty sure that what I felt in that moment was the same emotion Mookie felt in that middle school auditorium. It wasn't anger or even pain; both came later. More than anything, I just felt quizzical. I recognized in myself what I saw in his eyes all those years before. His eyes seemed to be asking, "What did I do to deserve that?" I had punched Mookie just as surely as that guy punched me.

I didn't hear the rest of his speech. I was too busy soaking in my own shame, the shame of seeing the worst part of yourself and knowing that somebody else has seen it too. A lot of people talk about how they grew up watching particular teams, particular ballplayers. But what I never knew is how deep that sentiment can run. Because that night, I really did grow up, at least a little, watching Mookie Wilson.

Jim Rice

MATT TAIBBI

Bill James ruined my childhood. Not my parents, not some girl who broke my heart in junior high, not drugs or alcohol or porn. Not any of those things, but Bill James. I hold the *Baseball Abstract* author and sometimes Red Sox consultant responsible for almost everything that has ever gone wrong in my life—and if I ever see him in person, I will set his beard on fire.

Up until the year 1983, when I turned thirteen and read *The Bill James Baseball Abstract* for the first time, I'd had my share of problems. My parents had gone through a messy divorce, and I had moved something like twelve times before junior high. I was pudgy, had a bad haircut and braces, and was one of the league leaders every school year in getting picked on by cool kids and laughed at by cute girls. I was the last kid to get picked up on my bus route, and when I got on every morning there was always one seat left open for me near the back—and on my way to it, each kid I passed would yell out, "Douche bag!" That was my life for most of junior high.

Throughout that time I had a hero. His name was Jim Rice. Jimmy had been my hero ever since I was a little boy. Like every kid from Massachusetts, I was a die-hard Red Sox fan. My father, a local TV reporter, sealed the deal when he took me to the famous Game Six of the 1975 World Series. I was five years old. Bernie Carbo's home run landed just a few rows in front of us. I still remember it; in the commotion in the bleachers caused by Carbo's blast, the thermos of hot chocolate my father had brought to the game was knocked over and my blue winter jacket got wet. The Fisk home run I actually don't remember. But I was a Sox fan for life after that.

I'm not sure where the attraction to Rice came from. I may have liked him simply because all the other kids were fans of white stars like Fred Lynn and Dewey Evans and Pudge. Rice didn't talk very much, and he always looked vaguely pissed off. There were all these stories about his legendary strength. I seem to remember one about him breaking a bat by checking his swing. I remember another game where a young boy in the stands got hit with a line drive and Jimmy carried him out of the park. Whenever the benches cleared in a Sox-game brawl, I used to love watching the crowd on the field part around Rice. He'd run in from left and the guys on the other team would mysteriously drift away from him in all directions, as if by accident. No one wanted any part of Jim Rice.

Lately, a great many sabermetricians—James disciples—have made great sport of laughing about Rice's reputation as the "most feared hitter" of his era. Quite obviously there is no way to quantify "feared"-ness, and even if one could do so somehow, it would just as obviously turn out to be irrelevant to winning baseball games, which of course is the point of the whole exercise.

But to a little kid like I was in the late '70s and early '80s, the fact that Rice was so feared was very important. And he was feared; I could see that pitchers were afraid of him. Not because they worried so much about him getting a hit at a key point in the game or avoiding somehow grounding into the crushing inning-ending double play (they weren't at all worried about that, as it turns out), but because they were afraid he would square one up and hit a line drive through their face. Or that he would mistake a pitch up and in for something it wasn't and end up at the mound. Rice wasn't feared for baseball reasons: His actual physical presence on the mound was feared.

And Jim Rice was scary. The fact that he had such a strained relationship with Boston and the Boston media made it that much easier for me to imagine him on my side; I wasn't getting along all that well with the Boston area either. Mentally I was probably bringing him along on the bus every day and imagining him dispensing justice, tossing all those asshole kids out the windows.

So imagine what it felt like for me when I opened up the *Baseball Abstract* at the age of thirteen and discovered that Jim Rice was, well, not all that good. Bill James introduced me to concepts like the GIDP (Rice hit a ton of those), OBP (he wasn't great there, either), and "range factor" (Rice was one of the worst outfielders). In a way the Bill James analytical method was a sort of revolution targeted directly at Jim Rice; James had taken aim at a statistical system that heavily favored misleading stats like batting average, outfield assists, and RBIs (Rice pluses) while severely discounting factors like strikeouts, double-play balls, walks, and chances (Rice minuses).

In the Jamesian view, Rice was a classically overrated ballplayer; a plodding slugger who struck out a lot, walked very seldom, fielded poorly, and played in a park that monstrously inflated his production to boot. The Jamesian method made players like Roy White look like better ballplayers than my avenging Jim Rice.

Reading James changed my view of baseball forever, and not in a good way. From 1983 through the end of Rice's career I started to notice cracks in the Rice edifice I had never noticed before. He seemed to hit a lot of home runs in the late innings of lopsided games. I also noticed, for the first time, what a bad combination hard-hit ground balls to short and lack of speed up the first-base line was. He was also hitting a lot of warning-track shots that would have been long gone before. The Rice of the late '70s and early '80s was a quick-twitch slugger who dented the Monster with ferocious line drives and sometimes hit ridiculously long homers. The Rice of the mid-'80s was an overblown singles hitter whose vision and knees were starting to fail him.

Worse still, Rice in the mid-'80s was in a batting order with two classic Bill James binkies—the later-stage, post–Charley Lau Dwight Evans and Wade Boggs. I could see what a dramatic effect it had on games when Boggs fought off so many pitches, and how Evans kept rallies alive with walks. Rice did not do these things. In fact, deep in my gut I knew that Rice's indifferent bat was a big reason why the Sox didn't close the deal in 1986, a World Series that set me back psychologically at least five years.

Rice's career ended with a whimper and ushered in one of the darker times in Red Sox history, a period that saw a parade of unpleasant, pull-happy goons like Jack Clark and Jose Canseco and Dante Bichette trotted out as pretenders to the hallowed title of Red Sox left fielder. The 1978 collapse, the 1986 loss, and the rise of Jamesian statistics seemed like a Holy Triumverate that would forever seal with disappointment the memory of my hero's career. It got worse with the fiasco that was Rice's Hall of Fame candidacy, when every James disciple worth his pocket protector crawled out of the woodwork, torches in hand, to rail against Rice's induction.

The suggestion that Rice's election would forever tarnish the Hall's legitimacy was particularly painful, especially since by that time I sort of agreed with them: Jim Rice, in the end, probably did not belong in the Hall of Fame. He just didn't play long enough. If his knees had held up a few more years, he'd have his 450 presteroid homers, and this Hall of Fame business wouldn't even be a discussion. But he didn't. And when he got in anyway at the eleventh hour, largely on the strength of efforts by the inconstant Boston media that once hated him, I actually felt embarrassed.

When I think about Jim Rice now, I think about how there are a lot of athletes whose lives and careers end up being dominated by things that exist far outside their area of expertise. Rice was just a regular blue-collar guy from South Carolina who knew how to play ball and naïvely thought that if he came to work every day and did his job that people would appreciate him. He just didn't understand why he was expected to stand in front of his locker after a good game and brag to reporters and go through the game all over again. "What am I supposed to say? 'I hit a hanging breaking ball?'" he complained once. I loved this about Jim Rice. It wasn't just that he wasn't full of shit; he didn't even understand how to be full of shit.

He played in a white man's town that worshiped white athletes like Fisk and Larry Bird, and there was always a little edge to every criticism leveled at him. And when the James revolution happened, and armies of stat geeks started taking the axe to Rice's career, there was a little edge there, too. It was just like white people to sit in their basements all winter pounding doughnuts and coming up with obscure formulas that showed why some black ballplayer wasn't as great as you thought he was when you watched him live, with your own eyes.

All of this was over Jimmy's head. He didn't handle it well; he didn't adapt. But that was fine with me, because I didn't handle being thirteen all that well either. The truth is that I rooted for Jim Rice more after I learned he wasn't that great. I wanted him to prove all of these materialist apostles of our hideously results-obsessed society wrong. I wanted him to make it to the big game and get the big hit and wipe away all the talk with one stroke.

He never did, but that's okay. Really, to hell with Bill James. Jim Rice may not have been great, but he was good enough. To me, anyway.

Mariano Rivera		◇	◇	◇	◇
DARIN STRAUSS					

When you freeze-frame on an insanely good pitcher in his motion—the elbow making a precise corner straight above the head, the back arched like a sail—you'll see something, an almost *Guinness Book*–ish anomaly. Something I'm only talented enough to describe as *extradexterous*.

Mariano Rivera is an insanely good pitcher. Watch him.* The arm is supple and boneless, like a whipped braid. But Rivera's body—even his arm—isn't *just* loose. The sinuous shoulder leads to the tensed hand. The great athletes look different, doing even the commonplace—having a catch, skipping across the boxing ring, bouncing a golf ball on the head of a nine-iron. Watch old Michael Jordan DVDs: See the poise and space-alien agility he shows just dribbling up the court. It's like when you notice Mariano quiet himself before a pitch. And then his body, midthrow, is all drawing-board angles. *Extradexterous* is a stupid word, probably.

---

* Here's a cool shot of what I'm talking about: http://ilovebubbadogs .com/bubbapress/wp-content/uploads/2007/11/rivera.jpg.

It's a downer to think about Mariano today. As I write this (the crack of the '09 season), the greatest relief pitcher ever has either started off with a few aberrant stinkeroos or has begun into a double-black-diamond decline; batters are going .293 against him, and he's given up four homers in his first eleven and one-third innings. (Four is the total of HRs he allowed all of last season.)

Anthony DiComo, of mlb.com:

> So rare are the occasions when Mariano Rivera blows a save that each hiccup prompts its own round of head-scratching. So imagine the scene in the Yankees' clubhouse after Thursday evening's game, when Rivera served up back-to-back home runs for the first time in his career.

Mariano* has a 3.91 ERA (so far) in 2009: unshabby for a mortal, but a hot turd compared even to Mariano's 2008, when he had a more Riverian 1.40 ERA and a ratio of 12.83 strikeouts for each walk he gave up—making him only the second pitcher since 1900 to be so accurate, so just about perfect. And compare today to all of 1996, when—in 107.2 innings—he gave up only one home run and logged twenty-six consecutive scoreless innings, including fifteen consecutive hitless frames. And compare *that* with his world-record career postseason ERA of 0.77, in 117.1 innings. (Most playoff appearances ever for a reliever, btw.) Or to the way he finished 1999 with forty-three consecutive scoreless innings. If I were a high school girl, I might phrase it: I have feelings for Mariano Rivera.

We don't usually ask, "How does someone remain so excellent for so long, at such a pressure-filled job?" Instead, it's, "How can this perfect

---

* And it's usually "Mariano" not "Rivera"—as it's usually "Kobe" not "Bryant," usually "Tiger" not "Woods."

____* machine falter?" Rivera is a skinny, impassive forty; he's been in the league fourteen years and has four World Series rings. He almost never fails. Or, rather, he's so often failed to fail—in a sport where success is sometimes defined as fucking up only two-thirds of the time— it's always kind of an upset if someone gets a hit off him; someone getting a *run* is an affront. In his championship years, Rivera's postseason ERA was 0.44. (That's going against only the best teams, only the real contenders, in the biggest games.) During his World Series run, Mariano gave up zero runs in eighteen playoff games. He has almost three times as many postseason saves as does number two on the all-time list, Hall of Famer Dennis Eckersley.

And so, Mariano Rivera this April is sad to watch, like a declining dogma.[†]

And there *is* something mythic about Mariano. In part, it's the sharp, imperturbable face, the frozen eyes; in part, his *Old Man and the Sea* bio (the fishing-boat childhood in Panama; the street-play apprenticeship, milk-carton gloves, tree-branch bats; the decision to try pro ball only after capsizing a 120-ton commercial boat; his having offered to move from shortstop to pitcher only when his Panama League team's ace was struggling as he's struggling now[§]).

----

* Relief-pitching, jump-shooting, putting—you name it, every sport's got one. But usually just one.[†]

[†] I was going to steer clear of David Foster Wallace–type footnotes in this essay, because they're practically a DFW trademark at this point, and no one wants to work another writer's (especially a great writer's) side of the street. But maybe because I've been thinking a lot about Wallace, too, and because I love his tennis writing—actually, all his writing, but the tennis stuff is what applies here—it seems pretty unavoidable.

[‡] I tire of the baseball/religion analogies, too. But every dogma has its own jargon, as V. S. Pritchett pointed out in his wonderful *The Saint*. And baseball is nothing if not jargon: WHIP, OPS, OBP, SLG, ZR.

[§] I'm not sure I can convey here, in a footnote, how much it hurts me even to write those words.

In part, it's that he's built his career, his dominance, on a single scrotum-tightener of a pitch: the cut fastball.* "[It was said that] this guy is going to have to come up with another pitch or he's not going to be able to stick around," Rivera's teammate Andy Pettitte told the *New York Times*. "Here we are, now he's the greatest closer ever and he's done it with one pitch." The massive home runner Jim Thome told the *Times* that Rivera's cutter is "the single best pitch ever in the game." But Rivera claimed in the New York *Daily News* that he discovered the cutter by accident, while playing catch with ex-Yankee Ramiro Mendoza. "It was just from God. I didn't do anything. It was natural."

In final part, the Mariano vibe springs from the Mariano demeanor. Most pitchers, even the most modest non–fist pumpers, glow a little after a big win. Or they do that hide-their-faces-in-their-gloves-and-scream thing when they give up an embarrassing hit. Mariano looks as robotically unperturbed giving up a home run as he does striking out the side in Game Seven of the ALCS.

There's something hard to define, something that separates this equanimity from the detachment I find so annoying in other players: in guys like A-Rod,† whose aloofness and chummy way with opponents—not to mention that salary—is a reminder, almost every time you see him, that all these players form an aristocracy, a guild of supercompetent mercenaries who care so much less about any "rivalry"

---

* Kind of like a fastball, but it breaks—i.e., it moves—when it crosses home plate. Think of the cutter as a half-curveball, half-fastball Frankenstein. Almost as fast as a straight fastball, with almost the movement of a curveball.

† And I kind of like A-Rod despite everything: the steroids, Madonna, the weird codependency with Derek Jeter, the strippers, the heinous salary, all of it. If you saw any of his 2007 season—AL-leading home runs (54), RBIs (156), slugging percentage (.645), OPS (1.067), total bases (376), and times on base (299), plus hitting .314 with ninety-five walks—you felt what it must have been like to watch Lou Gehrig. Plus, the game's best shortstop moved to third base and offered to take a pay cut to play for a winner.

than do the fans they're paid to stand for. That aristocratic guild includes Mariano, of course. But, I don't know. Mariano strikes me as being like the Bill Russell who sipped calming tea during practices but vomited before games; like the LeBron James who psyches himself up by hurling talc in the air before games to fill his arena with a puff of spectral powder. That is, he plays with so much attentiveness and *oomph* that he moves into some far-off mental real estate. What is self-consciously Zen-like in Russell, what is gloriously show-offy in LeBron, is in Mariano a shrinking of the universe, a placid concentration on the glove that waits exactly sixty feet six inches from his face. Yeah, I'm not sure I have the fortitude to keep writing this essay—because what does this wonderful man's decline portend for me?*

It is now a month later. Mariano in recent weeks had rebounded, it seems, and the Yankees have hopscotched from third place to first.

---

* Now, a lot of a-holes will point out here that Mariano did fail once in a big spot: Game Seven of the 2001 World Series.

Well...

In *The Last Night of the Yankee Dynasty* (sob!), Buster Olney writes about how a fast-moving little wind-and-rain storm swept in over the Arizona stadium, late in the game, causing a brief delay. Nobody on the Diamondbacks could ever recall seeing such a thing before. And, in fact, they hadn't. Apparently, these sorts of flash storms almost never occur before November—and of course, this World Series was the only one played in November, because of the interruption caused by 9/11.

As a result: Bottom of the ninth, Mariano is in his second inning of work because the overrated Joe Torre has refused to trust Ramiro Mendoza with the eighth, even though Mendoza had a 0.0 ERA in two innings against Arizona in the Series. After the first batter, Mark Grace, reaches base on a single, the second, Damian Miller, attempts to bunt but cracks the ball much too hard, right back at the mound. There's a good chance for a double play.

Two things that happen here: (1) The ball is wet from the rained-on grass (the grounds crew didn't do anything to guard the field from the quick storm), and Mariano's grip fails, making his throw to second wild; (2) The stupid,

But tonight he gave up four runs in the ninth to the Tampa Bay Rays. I turned off the TV before the fourth run, but with an increasing press on my heart I "watched" it online—not the broadcast game but the ticking changes to the box score; the slow patience of looking at shifting numbers felt like a suitable penance. But for what? Why do I, and many fans, feel that we're somehow culpable in our teams' losses? Why does it—this schoolyard game, played by men* who represent your city only nominally, and whose competition, when it comes down to it, has no tangible effect on either your life or your town—hurt so much?

I am thirty-nine years old—five months younger than Mariano. Of course, the bummer of this for me has partly to do with intimations of my own mortality, etc. Declines come quickly for athletes, making

---

throwback strip of dirt recently put in the Arizona stadium that runs from the pitcher's mound to the plate, Olney writes, causes the ball to come up more quickly than it would have in any other park, rolling up high on Mariano's glove, and as a result he rushes the throw to second.

Whatever the case, his throw draws Jeter off the bag, where he's spiked by Grace's pinch-runner, David Dellucci, and hurt so badly he thinks his foot is broken (he stays in the game). Then comes the second bunt, by Jay Bell. It's also botched, and this time Mo throws to third in time to get Dellucci. But Yankee third baseman Scott Brosius never throws back to first, where he could have gotten a DP. Then the trapdoor opens: a weird broken-bat double, a Luis Gonzalez little pop fly. (According to Keith Olbermann, who was there as a sportscaster, Torre had the outfield positioned wrongly, and the Gonzalez hit should have been caught.)

The real key, though, was the first bunt. If it *is* a double play, all Rivera has to do then is get Bell, an aging bench player. Disgusting. Anyway, see that it was a fluky confluence of events, and never in there did Mariano make a bad pitch, and no one got a solid hit off him.

* This is the thing that seems weirdest—the men playing a boys' game— when you go to the stadium and have really, really good seats. On TV it seems like theater; ten feet from a grown man wearing a Little League outfit, it seems a bit ludicrous. More on this later.

them the perfect symbol for our own fallings off—you may age slowly, but when you look back, it seems only yesterday you were a carefree young guy, and not lifting children with what Martin Amis calls barking spines and hysterical knees.

It's more than that, of course. Young men feel the pain of a loss, too—I've seen a tenth-grader (okay, me) crying about a blown save in the presence of an older person (okay, my father) who seemed only slightly more successful at keeping his emotions in restraint.

There are two reasons for this, I think.

1. Sports are set up to allow us to experience failure somewhat healthily. One team in thirty wins it all—and that's only in pro baseball; how many colleges vie for the NCAA title?—and so it's like a steam valve for our real problems; it allows us to work off our upset about trivial things, so we don't have to get pissed about the real problems in our own lives. Which leads me to:

2. It's a cliché that men—often fathers and sons—talk about sports because they may have little else to talk about. It gives them a conversation topic. But what's less known—at least I've never heard it acknowledged—is that sports make up the only space where it's okay for men to show their feelings openly to one another. Again, this may be due to the distance from the stressing mortgages and cold breakfasts of our real lives; it's not cool to bawl when your girlfriend leaves you, but it's fine to devote real emotional suffering to the outcome of a game, played by men you'll never know, who would probably not like you if you did know them, and vice versa, because they're mostly egomaniacal multimillionaires who've had no education or socializing influence in their lives. And it's not some ironic devotion—we fans don't pretend to care about this stuff; we do, passionately and for real.

I've seen a fat and drunk guy with what I thought was a White Power tattoo take a lawyerly black woman into a hug outside the bleachers of Yankee Stadium. I've seen a young man (okay, me again) look daggers at his girlfriend for a whole night because she made him miss the game where John Starks dunked on Jordan. I've seen an older, pious-looking man with Hasidic sidecurls curse and spit at a referee. None of this seemed weird to me. I had friends in high school who were inarticulate about everything—their own feelings, the stuff they were supposed to be studying, what they thought about a book or movie or song or girl—but who had sharp-eyed insights about the minutiae of sport and could express these both poetically and without fear of being teased: the cool *tunk* of the hardball off an aluminum bat; why refs were more likely to blow a whistle against away teams (the obvious factor of intimidation, and also the subtler, subconscious desire simply not to be hated); the way managers were incorrectly balancing the needs of winning a single game with those of running the long campaign of a full season.

I think the reason that sports often don't appeal to people who were picked on (and I say this as someone who knows what it's like) is that those people have, often correctly, developed the congenital sense that life is unfair; that their being picked on has nothing to do with any of their own real shortcomings, but is due rather to the vagaries of life. That's why so many geeks and ex-geeks find solace in irony. See the hipsters in, say, Williamsburg (and what is a New York hipster but a reformed nerd from somewhere else?) in their "Vinny" gas station attendant shirts. Punk rock, alternative film, literary fiction, even the better cable TV shows—these are all drenched in irony. Which is a good thing. A lot of capital-A Art should be ironic.

Sports, however, are irony-free. That's why there are so few really artful—as opposed to stirring—sports movies. *Field of Dreams* will make me cry every time, but it's a dumb, sentimental movie, if you think about it. Sports are shot through with certainty (whereas so little in life, or Art, is certain). They reward hard work. Success and failure—like the categories *skilled* and *unskilled*—are accurately quantified. You can argue a call here or there, but you can't argue against career stats. And there are no mixed reviews: Everyone knows what determines quality.

What's more, as Nietzsche pointed out, we like sports because they show us beauty and perfection. (And that's part of why I love Mariano; he's too graceful not to love.) Sports show us, too, the primacy of strength and beauty and—yes—youth. It's wish fulfillment; we can better face the PowerPoint presentations and stale danishes of our workaday lives when we imagine ourselves pitching in the bottom of the ninth of Game Seven. There's nothing "carpe diem" about most of our existences. But when you see people giving the lie to human imperfection, you feel a little part of that, too.

Which I guess—this has taken me pretty far afield here—brings me back to Mariano. The joy he's given me is the joy I used to feel reading *Superman* comics as a kid. Maybe the reason I've liked Mariano—more than, say, the slobbishly human David Wells or the smiling and savvy Robinson Cano, the deep-digging Andy Pettitte or the lovable, self-proclaimed idiot Johnny Damon—is the same reason I liked the invulnerable Superman and not the scrappy and all-too-human Batman (though even as a kid I knew Batman had better art and story lines). I want my heroes to be fully heroic, fully untouchable.*

---

* All the same, some might say this also makes it hard to love Mariano. Do you love Spock; do you love a robot? People certainly relate better to the endearingly coarse Red Sox team that broke the curse than to the smoothly professional '98 Yankee team that won 125 games.†

  † Since we're mentioning the Red Sox, let me state here my disgust with the whole anti-Yankees bigotry that's so prevalent across baseball fandom. Why do Yankee supporters have to apologize for rooting for a winner? What fan wouldn't want her team's owner to be Steinbrennerian—to be

I think that's also why I like watching the games on TV better than in person, even when I have great seats. This gets at, I think, one of the paradoxes of TV. You'd think that the intimacy of TV would bring the game down to a human dimension, whereas sitting in the bleachers, six hundred feet from the action, would sort of mythologize it. It should be kind of like *Pomp* versus *Being Able, During Close-Ups, to See Someone's Zits*. But the reality is the opposite—TV-enabled closeness to the action brings the opposite of intimacy. Maybe it's because my generation is more comfortable seeing our myths on a flatscreen. But it's a movielike experience, watching a game projected by cathode rays. It doesn't seem like it's just a bunch of guys playing ball.[‡]

Anyway, so I'm not sure any of the above makes sense. Extradextrousness, dogmas in decline, and all the rest of it. You can go on and on about baseball, because there's no end to it—the oceans of stats, the huge community of fans, the overwhelming history that makes it seem centuries older than basketball and football. But if you go on too

---

someone willing to pay (or overpay) to win? George is often dumb and rash, but he sure beats most teams' corporate owners, oligarchs who care less if their team wins than if it makes money. Anyone who thinks she's being virtuous by rooting for a shitty team should find some more worthy receptacle for her righteousness—a monastery, perhaps, or a Greenpeace antiwhaling barge.

[‡] The best comparison I have is boxing. I loved boxing as a kid, and my first story as a journalist was to interview Larry Holmes in the mid-'90s, when he was trying to make a comeback. It was a thrill to meet him. He was great and nice and charismatic, and I got the feeling that he'd have been a much bigger star if he hadn't been screwed by fate by being the champion to follow directly after the unearthly charismatic Muhammad Ali. But then, when I watched the fight from the press seats, all the theater and beauty of boxing left. What replaced it was the feeling that I was watching two big guys slugging the shit out of each other. It was gross and sad, and I wanted to jump up, as you would do, and stop my new friend from getting his face punched in.

much, it starts to mean nothing. That is, I've written above that geeks don't like sports and then compared athletes to Superman. So, yeah, I've had trouble with this essay, because the subject matter—the slow fall of Mariano—vibrates right in my pain frequency. I guess it just comes down to this: So far this year it's been hard watching him. It's hard to make heroes out of strangers who play for a living. I want to stop caring. I want not to feel slightly nauseated after a bad loss. I want to stop watching 162 four-hour games a year. I've tried above to figure out why we care so much, but I don't know if I ever really will. If Mariano is really Superman, then his kryptonite—as it is for all of us real-life Clark Kents—is time.

CONTRIBUTORS' NOTES

John Albert grew up in Los Angeles. As a teenager, he cofounded the cross-dressing "death rock" band Christian Death, then played drums for the seminal punk band Bad Religion. He has written for the *Los Angeles Times, LA Weekly, BlackBook, Fader,* and *Hustler,* among others; won awards for sports and arts journalism; and appeared in several national anthologies. His book *Wrecking Crew* (Scribner's), chronicling the true-life adventures of his amateur baseball team made up of drug addicts, transvestites, and washed-up rock stars, has been optioned by studios three times so far.

Steve Almond is the author of five books, none of them quite as good as he'd hoped. He lives outside Boston with his wife and two children, and still roots for the Oakland A's against his better judgment.

Buzz Bissinger is the author of *Friday Night Lights, Three Nights in August,* and *Shooting Stars,* coauthored with LeBron James.

Michael Ian Black has starred in noted television series and films including *Michael & Michael Have Issues, Stella, The State, Wet Hot American Summer, Viva Variety,* Vh1's *I Love the . . .* series, and NBC's *Ed.* He wrote the screenplay for *Run Fatboy Run,* wrote and directed the film *Wedding Daze,* and is the author of *My Custom Van: And 50 Other Mind-Blowing Essays That Will Blow Your Mind All over Your Face* and the children's book *Chicken Cheeks.* He lives in Connecticut with his wife and two kids.

Jim Bouton is a former Yankee pitcher, author of *Ball Four,* and a veteran Met League player. As sources for his essay, he thanks Jay Horowitz, Stan Isaacs, Jerry Izenberg, Kevin Kernan, Russ Mensch, and John Szczygiel.

Jonathan Eig is the author of two best-selling books, *Luckiest Man: The Life and Death of Lou Gehrig* and *Opening Day: The Story of Jackie Robinson's First Season*. He is working on a book about Al Capone that will be published in the spring of 2010.

Stefan Fatsis is the author of three books: *A Few Seconds of Panic: A Sportswriter Plays in the NFL*; *Word Freak: Heartbreak, Triumph, Genius, and Obsession in the World of Competitive Scrabble Players*; and *Wild and Outside: How a Renegade Minor League Revived the Spirit of Baseball in America's Heartland*. He talks about sports on NPR's *All Things Considered,* and writes a column for Sports Illustrated.com. His work also has appeared in the *Wall Street Journal*, the *New York Times*, the *Washington Post, Sports Illustrated, Atlantic Monthly, Slate,* and other publications.

Craig Finn is the singer and lyricist for the Hold Steady. He lives in Brooklyn and every day gets a little bit more obsessed with the Minnesota Twins.

Doug Glanville was selected in the first round of the 1991 amateur draft by the Chicago Cubs. His professional baseball career spanned fifteen seasons, nine at the major-league level with the Cubs, Philadelphia Phillies and Texas Rangers. He has contributed to ESPN.com, serves as the Cubs expert for Chicago Sports Webio, and writes a regular column for the *New York Times* titled "Heading Home." His first book, an account of a year in the life of major-league players, will be published by Times Books in the spring of 2010.

Pat Jordan is a contract writer with the *New York Times Magazine* and the author of the memoirs *A False Spring* and *A Nice Tuesday*. His most recent book is a collection of his sports profiles, *The Best Sports Writing of Pat Jordan* (Persea Books).

Roger Kahn has often been called the best baseball writer in the country. He earned national celebrity in 1972 with the publication of his book *The Boys of Summer,* which has sold nearly 3 million copies and is in its eighty-fifth printing. Kahn is the author of twenty books and hundreds of articles in national magazines such as *Esquire, Sports Illustrated, Time,* and the *Saturday Evening Post*. His most recent book is *Into My Own: The Remarkable People and Events That Shaped a Life.*

King Kaufman wrote a daily sports column for *Salon* from 2002 to 2009. He lives in San Francisco and is the commissioner of the Scoresheet simulation baseball league N.L. Neifi.

W. P. Kinsella has published thirty-some books and hundreds of short stories, articles, reviews, and poems. He is best known for the novel *Shoeless Joe,* which became the basis for the movie *Field of Dreams*. Among his honors are the Order of Canada, the Order of BC, the Stephen Leacock Medal for Humor, and the George Woodcock Lifetime Achievement Award for Fiction.

Laura Lippman has published fifteen crime novels and a collection of short stories. Her work includes the prize-winning Tess Monaghan series and several stand-alone novels, including the *New York Times* best-seller *What the Dead Know*. She lives in Baltimore.

Sean Manning is editor of the anthologies *The Show I'll Never Forget: 50 Writers Relive Their Most Memorable Concertgoing Experience* and *Rock and Roll Cage Match: Music's Greatest Rivalries, Decided*. His writing has appeared in *New York Press, Black-Book,* and the *Brooklyn Rail*.

Seth Mnookin is a contributing editor at *Vanity Fair*. He began his career as a rock and jazz critic, and has worked for the *Palm Beach Post, Newsweek,* and the *Forward*. He is the author of the 2006 *New York Times* best-seller *Feeding the Monster,* which chronicles the year he spent with the Boston Red Sox and the remaking of the team into a World Series winner. He also wrote *Hard News,* a 2004 *Washington Post* Best Book of the Year, which is about the media and, despite having absolutely nothing to do with baseball, is quite interesting and enjoyable. He is working on a book about vaccines.

Whitney Pastorek is a writer, musician, and international star of stage and screen who spent the last five and a half years as a staff writer at *Entertainment Weekly*. Other credits include *ESPN: The Magazine, Sports Illustrated,* the *Village Voice,* the *New York Times,* and a 2008 essay collection very similar to this one called *Rock and Roll Cage Match* (Whitney versus Mariah—Whitney wins). She continues to be executive editor of a literary magazine called *Pindeldyboz,* is unapologetically based in Los Angeles, and will get whittlz.com back online someday.

Jeff Pearlman is a former *Sports Illustrated* senior baseball writer and the *New York Times* best-selling author of four books, including *The Bad Guys Won!* and *Boys Will Be Boys*. He blogs at www.jeffpearlman.com.

Neal Pollack is the author of several books of satirical fiction and the best-selling memoir *Alternadad*. He contributes to many publications, including *Men's Journal, Maxim,* the *New York Times Magazine,* and *Slate*. His next book, *Yoga Dork,* will be published in spring 2010 by Harper Perennial. A lifelong Dodger fan, Pollack lives in Los Angeles with his family.

Scott Raab has been a writer at large for *Esquire* since 1997. Born and raised in Cleveland, he is a graduate of Cleveland State University and the University of Iowa's Writer's Workshop. He lives in New Jersey.

Carrie Rickey is a film critic for the *Philadelphia Inquirer*. For many years she resisted switching her allegiance from the Dodgers. She converted to the Phillies in 1993 when portly first baseman John Kruk told a fan, "I ain't no athlete, lady. I'm a baseball player."

Esmaralda Santiago is the author of three acclaimed memoirs: *When I Was Puerto Rican, Almost a Woman,* and *The Turkish Lover.* She's also a novelist, essayist, and screenwriter. She and her filmmaker husband, Frank Cantor, live in Westchester County, New York.

Christopher Sorrentino is the author of three novels, including *Trance,* a finalist for the National Book Award in 2005. His work has appeared in *Esquire, Harper's,* the *New York Times, Playboy, Tin House,* and numerous other publications.

Darin Strauss is the international best-selling author of the *New York Times* Notable Books *Chang and Eng* and *The Real McCoy,* and the national best-seller *More Than It Hurts You.* The recipient of a 2006 Guggenheim Fellowship in fiction writing, he is a clinical associate professor at New York University's creative writing program.

Matt Taibbi is a contributing editor for *Rolling Stone* and winner of the 2007 National Magazine Award for Columns and Commentary. He is the author of *The Great Derangement: A Terrifying True Story of War, Politics, and Religion; Smells Like Dead Elephants: Dispatches from a Rotting Empire;* and *Spanking the Donkey: Dispatches from the Dumb Season.*

Robert Whiting is the Western world's foremost authority on Japanese baseball and author of the classic *You Gotta Have Wa* (an updated and expanded version of which was released in 2009). His other works include *The Chrysanthemum and the Bat, The Samurai Way of Baseball: The Impact of Ichiro and the New Wave from Japan,* and *Tokyo Underworld: The Fast Times and Hard Life of an American Gangster in Japan.* He has written for the *New York Times, Sports Illustrated, Newsweek,* and *Time,* among other publications. He lives in Tokyo.

CONTRIBUTORS' CREDITS

ACKNOWLEDGMENTS

For their help and encouragement, the editor thanks Jim Fitzgerald (*Jim Rice*); Jonathan Crowe (*Terry Pendleton*), John Radziewicz (*Bill Lee*), Lissa Warren (*Reggie Jackson*), Renee Caputo (*Cal Ripken Jr.*), Mark Sorkin (*Ryne Sandberg*), and everyone involved at Da Capo Press; Vanessa White Wolf (*Sean Manning*); James Manning (*Mickey Mantle*); and Susan Manning (*tie: Sean Manning, Jim Thome*).